The Italian American Experience

OUR ITALIAN
FELLOW CITIZENS

In Their Old Homes and Their New

FRANCIS E. CLARK

ARNO PRESS

A New York Times Company

New York — 1975

Reprint Edition 1975 by Arno Press Inc.

Reprinted from a copy in The Princeton
  University Library

The Italian American Experience
ISBN for complete set: 0-405-06390-3
See last pages of this volume for titles.

Manufactured in the United States of America

———◆———

Library of Congress Cataloging in Publication Data

Clark, Francis Edward, 1851-1927.
    Our Italian fellow citizens in their old homes and
their new.

    (The Italian American experience)
    Reprint of the ed. published by Small, Maynard, Bos-
ton.
    1. Italian Americans. 2. Americanization. I. Ti-
tle. II. Series.
E184.I8C5 1975   917.3'06'51   74-17923
ISBN 0-405-06396-2

OUR ITALIAN FELLOW CITIZENS

Venice — the Campanile, St. Marks and the Doges' Palace

OUR ITALIAN FELLOW CITIZENS

In Their Old Homes and Their New

BY

FRANCIS E. CLARK, D.D., LL.D.

Author of "Old Homes of New Americans," "The
Holy Land of Asia Minor," "The Continent
of Opportunity," "Christian Endeavor
in all Lands," etc., etc.

BOSTON
SMALL, MAYNARD & COMPANY
PUBLISHERS

140523

INTRODUCTION

One of the most interesting of the allied countries in the recent world war is that narrow, bootlegged peninsula which juts out into the Mediterranean and forms the eastern shore of the Adriatic. In its history it is the most fascinating country in the world. In its contribution to arts and letters it is unsurpassed. The ancient Romans gave laws not only to Italy but to all the world, and these laws are still in force.

The modern Italian has shown himself as intrepid in war, and as resourceful in overcoming difficulties, as the legionaries of ancient Rome.

Italy is of peculiar interest, not only because we were associated with her in the recent earth-shaking crisis, but because she has sent so many millions of her sons to our shores, and is likely to send millions more now that Peace broods over a tortured world, and because the Italian admixture will profoundly affect our national life, and our racial characteristics.

My purpose in this volume is chiefly to make my readers sympathetically acquainted, so far as I am able, with the Italian of to-day in his old home and his new.

For this purpose I have not only studied his history and his achievements in the past, but I have tried through personal acquaintance to understand something of his present viewpoint. In a word, I have sought to introduce him as he is to my fellow Americans who trace their descent from other racial stocks. This volume was largely written in Italy, while the places and people described were freshly in mind.

The ignorance and brutal indifference of many Americans to the newcomer who seeks our shores is often amazing. They are all "Dagoes" to him, the "Scum of the Earth," as Mr. Schauffler entitles his remarkable poem. It is difficult to disabuse the minds of some Americans of the idea that the immigrants are "a horde of paupers and criminals," while, as a matter of fact, there are fewer of these classes allowed to land on our shores than can be found among any similar number of people in any state of the Union.

I have long felt that the cure for this astonishing ignorance and indifference toward the immigrant is simply larger information and better acquaintance with him. This larger knowledge and better acquaintance will show us, not only that he is a human being of like passions with ourselves, but that he has many admirable and redeeming traits of character which we may well imitate; that he will respond to kindly and generous treatment, as will few other people, for his loneliness and isolation make him peculiarly open to friendly advances. A little first-hand knowledge, or second-hand, if the former is unavailable, will teach us that the average immigrant has in him the qualities which will make an admirable citizen, and we shall no longer dismiss him contemptuously as a "Dago" or a "Wop," but will see in him not only a man and brother, but a future fellow citizen, who himself, or through his descendants, may contribute greatly to the welfare and prosperity of our country.

Especially is all this true of the Italian immigrant, and while I have striven to avoid becoming his eulogist, I have tried to look upon him with a sympathetic eye, and to induce the sympathy and regard of others. I have briefly rehearsed the glorious history which lies behind every Italian, and which is the necessary background of our picture, but especially have I endeavored, as best I could, to depict him in his home, in the country or city, to show his virtues as well as to point out his failings and foibles.

In considering Italy and the Italian, we must never forget that his is practically a new nation. Scarcely more than fifty years ago Italy did not exist, the Italian Peninsula was occupied by a

number of warring, turbulent, mutually jealous
and suspicious states, and as a result of this state
of practical anarchy, ignorance, violence and
degradation followed. A country, which in fifty
years can make out of this conglomerate mass of
hostile elements a first-class, flourishing European Power, must possess citizens of no mean
qualities of heart and mind. Still, after less than
two generations of freedom and unity, we cannot
expect perfection either in the nation or in the
individuals who compose it.

Mr. Arthur H. Norway in his interesting book
"Naples Past and Present" puts the matter ad-
mirbaly when he writes:

The most careless of observers can see that
some things still go wrong in Italy; that the
Italians are not yet wholly made; and it is the
easiest, as it is the stupidest of tasks, to demon-
strate that forty years of freedom have not taught
the youngest nation what the oldest took eight
centuries to learn. It galls me to hear the super-
cilious remarks dropped by strangers coming
from a country where serious difficulties of government have not existed in the memory of man,
the casual wisdom of critics who look around too
carelessly to note the energy with which, one by
one, the roots of evil are plucked up, and the
refuse of the long tyranny cleared away.

I am not writing a political tract, but I say

once for all that the recent history of Italy can show more triumphs than failures; and the day will surely come when the indomitable courage of her rulers shall purge the country of those cankers which for centuries ate out her manhood.

To present to the best of my ability a first hand report of this remarkable people, I have journeyed from southern Sicily to the Waldensian Valleys, from Syracuse to Turin, have seen the Italians in country and city, and have lived, sometimes for months at a time, within their borders, with the view of presenting to my readers a fair, unprejudiced, but sympathetic account of the millions of men with Italian blood who are in our midst, and of the millions more who are yet to come.

What effect in the long future the war of the nations may have upon Italy, or indeed upon any of the belligerent countries, no one is wise enough to predict, but it is entirely probable that it will draw our own nation and the land of the ancient Romans more closely together in sympathetic and commercial ties. It may hasten many more of Italy's sons to our shores. In any event, it makes it the more imperative that we should understand them, through a study of their history, their recent development, and their racial characteristics.

CONTENTS

CONTENTS

ILLUSTRATIONS

OUR ITALIAN FELLOW CITIZENS

CHAPTER I

ITALY AND AMERICA

In the first ten years of this century more than 2,300,000 emigrants sailed for our shores from Italy alone. During the first decade of the twentieth century something like one forty-fifth of all the people now in the United States had left their sunny fatherland and crossed the wide ocean for the continent discovered by an Italian more than four centuries earlier. When we consider the multitude of Italians who had made our republic their home during the last century, when we remember the millions of children who have been born and will yet be born to these immigrants, down to the third and fourth generation, for there is no race suicide in this branch of the Latin family, we can begin to realize in some degree how profoundly these people will influence the future of America, and how important it is that Americans should gain a just and sympathetic knowledge of the peaceful hordes which have invaded and will invade this Promised Land.

What a marvellous little country is this peninsula of Italy, little, comparatively, in territory, but filling more pages of the world's history than any other land since the dawn of letters! So many mighty events have been packed into the story of this peninsula that it is hard for an American to realize how comparatively small is its area. Not counting Italia Irredenta, 110,675 square miles measured the extent of modern Italy, just twenty-five miles less than the area of our desert state of Nevada, while New Mexico, Arizona and Montana all exceed it in size. California is nearly half as large again, while into Texas two kingdoms of Italy could be packed, with a wide margin around the borders of both. Half a dozen other states, like Colorado, Oregon, Wyoming, Idaho and South Dakota approximate Italy in size.

Yet this state, so comparatively small, is mighty in deeds of valor and statesmanship, in art and letters and invention and discovery. It has given its laws to the remotest regions of the world; it has dictated its canons of painting and sculpture and music and poetry to all the capitals of Europe. It has led in the means of inter-communication which bind the nations together.

Its early emperors taught the world how to build roads and bridges which have never been surpassed in the later centuries. It sent out Columbus to explore the watery main beyond the Pillars of Hercules, and to bind the new world to the old, and last of all, even in our own century, the Italian Marconi has made electricity his servant, to complete the work of Columbus, and to bring the ends of the earth together by the highway of the invisible ether.

Before the war the bone and sinew of this country, the hard working peasantry of this marvellous land, flocked to our shores in larger numbers than from any other.

What study, then, can be more interesting or valuable to Americans than the history and progress, and particularly the social conditions of this people?

The task of outlining their history, and describing such a people in a succinct and readable style is enough to appal any writer, and to merit the sympathy of any reader. Yet it is a task worth attempting if, thereby, any considerable number of Americans may become better acquainted with, and more sympathetically inclined towards these fellow citizens, whose influence for weal or woe upon the future destinies of our country cannot be measured.

The Italians differ from the other great races of the modern world in being more versatile in their abilities and their achievements. The poorest Italian emigrant is by blood and language linked with conquerors and rulers, great administrators, artists, musicians and poets. Other important races of the world are distinguished for superiority in some one or two or three lines of achievement. The Greeks were artists and poets and orators, but they were never great administrators or rulers, at least after the earlier days of their national glory. The British have distinguished themselves in the field of administration and colonization, but they are not supreme as artists; the Germans are philosophers and have been considered men of might in war and diplomacy, but they have not the many-sidedness of the Italian character.

Moreover the Italians show great recuperative power. They have been defeated, but never annihilated, as were some of the great nations of the ancient world. They have suffered innumerable reverses from foes within and foes without, but the recent renaissance of Italy, which after centuries of comparative feebleness and decay has placed her once more among the great powers of Europe, shows the resiliency of the Latin nature.

At the present moment, the common people of Italy seem to be coming for the first time into their full inheritance. No longer are they the serfs of the Cæsars, to be cajoled with games and bribes of corn to keep the peace, as was the case in the days of Nero and other emperors, when it is said that one half of the millions of Rome were really paupers, fed at the public expense from the great storehouses of grain which lined the banks of the Tiber.

As I write this first chapter of my book in the heart of Italy's capital, a sympathetic strike is going on, which has stopped every tram-car wheel in Rome, and sent every public cab to the stables, and shut up every shop along the busy streets, with the exception of apothecary shops and the restaurants. And what is the reason for this absolute cessation of trade and traffic, on this bright, spring day? Simply that the government has closed one of the public hospitals and cab drivers and street-car men, draymen and clerks are showing their disapproval by a strike which may last for a day or a week, or until their grievance is redressed.

Whatever may be the merits of this particular strike, of which a foreigner is not in a position to judge, it at least shows the marvellous strides which modern Italy has made in the assertion of the rights of the common people, and indicates how long a road has been travelled, not only since the days of the Cæsars and of the Guelphs and Ghibellines, but even since Mazzini and Cavour and Garibaldi first raised the banner of a United Italy. Surely the story of such a people, which sent every day for years almost a thousand people to our shores, should be of extreme interest to every American.

The earliest inhabitants of Italy who are recorded in history were related to the Greeks, and were of the same Aryan race, though having distinct qualities and characteristics of their own; while in the south of Italy, especially, were pure Greek colonies at a very early date. Space does not permit me to speak particularly of the Etruscans, Ligurians, Venetians, and the Celtic tribes which in the early days occupied different parts of the long peninsula, but it is interesting to know that the Italians, like all the great races of the world, have mixed blood flowing in their veins.

Greek and Celt and Norman, and Spaniard and Saracen and the barbarians from beyond the Alps have from time to time sent their hordes to devastate fair Italy, and, whether conquered or conquering, have in time been assimilated, and become as good Italians as those of purest blood. In this respect the history of Italy has been not unlike our own. America is no longer English though we speak the English language. Saxon, Celt and Gaul, Teuton and Slav, Magyar and Syrian, and last, but by no means the least, the Italian has come to help form the cosmopolitan American character.

For more than two thousand five hundred years Rome has been, except for brief intervals, the ruling power of Italy. The year 753 before Christ is a date which every school boy knows, and is one of the great years in the world's history, for it is the generally accepted date of the founding of the Imperial City. From this event for a thousand years the whole civilized world dated its letters and its documents. "As the years went on, all the little settlements on the neighboring hills were walled in as one city, with Rome as the largest, ruling over all Latium, and from this time Rome continued to increase in power and influence, first by conquering and annexing many peoples, and then by giving laws to these people."

It is, of course, impossible to tell here the story of the Roman Empire, nor is it necessary for our purpose. It has been well said that, "The history of Europe is almost wholly made up, first of the steps by which the older states came under the power of Rome, and secondly of the way in which the modern states of Europe were formed by the breaking up of that power."

We all know how the early kingdom of Rome, which lasted from the foundation of the city to the beginning of the fifth century before Christ, was succeeded by a republic which lasted for half a millennium until very near the beginning of the Christian Era.   It is interesting to remember that the decisive battle between the republicans under Brutus and Cassius, and the monarchists under Mark Antony and Octavius Cæsar, was fought on the Plain of Philippi, and that on the hillside near by was the Roman city where Paul and Silas were imprisoned, and to whose Christians the great Apostle wrote his Epistle to the Philippians.   It will be remembered also that the republican army started from Sardis, the ancient city of Crœsus, one of the Seven Cities, to which the messages of the Book of Revelation were sent, and marched across the mountains to their disastrous defeat at Philippi.   Thus all the way along the great events of the early days of Christianity are interwoven with the great events of the history of Rome.

Nor must we forget that it was the splendid Roman roads and bridges that made it possible for Paul and Peter and the early disciples to carry the news of Christianity into all parts of the known world. It was the might and justice of the Roman power which enabled Paul for years to escape the wrath of the Jews, though barely with his life, in Corinth, and Thessalonica, in Iconium and Lystra and Philippi, in Jerusalem and Cesarea, and thus he was enabled to carry out those marvellous missionary journeys which resulted in planting the new religion throughout the Roman Empire and the then known world.

Indeed the later history of Christianity is hardly less identified with Italy than these earlier days. Sometimes it has been a Christianity of a corrupt and intolerant character, but never has Rome ceased to exercise a profound influence upon the religion, as well as upon the manners and morals of the world.

I need not allude to the long story of the emperors, good, bad and indifferent, who, from the time of the Battle of Philippi, for five hundred years ruled the world. Little by little the great nation extended its power. France, Spain, Great Britain saw her conquering armies, and bowed before her might; the Latin language became well nigh universal, and the manners and customs of the Romans became the manners and customs of civilization.

But Rome was not satisfied with conquering

and ruling Europe alone.   In Asia all the land west of the Euphrates, and in Africa all the land north of the Great Desert, was ruled by Romans in the height of her power, and the eagle of the Cæsars was everywhere the symbol of all-conquering might and usually of law and order and a just and righteous form of government.

CHAPTER II

For more than a thousand years, Rome as a kingdom, as a republic, as an empire, was practically ruler of the world, patron of the arts and sciences, maker of laws for all nations, and arbiter of their destinies. Then came a period of about the same length, something over a thousand years, when she was the football of the nations, buffeted and kicked and beaten by Huns and Vandals and Moors, by Ostrogoths and Visigoths, by heathen Lombards from Hungary and by the Byzantine Exarchs from Constantinople.

During these dark years a few dates in her history are memorable. One was the year 800, when Charlemagne, the son of Pepin of France, the mighty warrior and administrator, was crowned "Emperor of the West" by Pope Leo III, in St. Peter's Cathedral.

To pay Leo for his crown, Charlemagne gave to the Church Spoleto, a city situated about half way between Rome and Florence. We are told

by the guide books that the present peaceful and
prosaic occupation of its inhabitants is the gathering of mushrooms in the woods nearby and the
preserving of fruits and vegetables for the
market. Humdrum as this little city is to-day,
its gift to Leo by Charlemagne was the unfor-
tunate beginning of the temporal power of the
Church of Rome, which lasted for a thousand
years and more, even down to our own times,
and proved disastrous to the spiritual welfare
of the church as many Catholics as well as most
Protestants believe, by creating a great, powerful, and sometimes corrupt hierarchy.

Charlemagne, however, could not transmit his
great qualities to his descendants. Three of his
grandsons were his heirs, and the great empire
over which he ruled, consisting of Italy, France
and Germany, was divided among them. Italy
fell to the lot of Lothair, but later was merged,
under Otto the Great of Germany, into the *Holy
Roman Empire of the German Nation.*

The long and bitter quarrel between the
Guelphs and Ghibellines now began. The Ghibellines sided with the emperors and the Guelphs
with the Popes. This is really the quarrel which,
in one form or another, continued until 1870,
when Victor Emanuel marched triumphantly into
Rome, through the street now called *Via Venti*

The Christopher Columbus House in Genoa

Settembre, as King of United Italy. This event was so comparatively recent that we can still almost hear the rejoicing shouts of the people, and see their hats tossed high in air as they realized that once more, after the long, long centuries of defeat and disaster, Italy was again free and united.

Other great names must not be entirely omitted in this review of the salient points of Italian history. Frederick Barbarossa (Frederic of the Red Beard), a German Prince, became king of Italy in the latter part of the twelfth century. Resenting his rule, twenty-three Italian cities rebelled against him and formed the Lombard League, which at last triumphed, and compelled Barbarossa to allow them to govern themselves.

The story of these city republics is most interesting, and each one, if told in detail, would fill many volumes. Genoa, Pisa, Venice and Florence, each, in turn, was the conqueror or the conquered, but each one sought its own glory and preëminence, and none cared for the glory of a united Italy. The Crusades brought great riches to some of these cities. Venice particularly prospered, at one time being mistress not only of most of Italy, but of half the old Roman Empire.

These ages of war and turmoil and adventure,

of city pitted against city, when Italy was torn by factions and quarrels of all kinds, was, strange as it may seem, the age of her greatest literary and artistic glory.   During these years Dante and Petrarch wrote, Cimabue set new ideals before all modern painters, and Giotto built his wonderful cathedral and campanile.

Corrupt as were many of the ecclesiastical and political rulers, reformers and men of eminent piety were not wanting, perhaps raised up and made eloquent and powerful by their revolt against the corruption of the age.   It is only necessary to mention the names of St. Francis and Savonarola to prove this, and to prove also the virile, unconquerable strain always found in the Italian character even in Italy's most decadent days.

An event of peculiar interest to Americans occurred in Genoa in 1435, for then a little boy was born to Dominico and Susanna Colombo, a son whom they named Cristoforo, or the Christ-bearer, an unconscious prophecy, perhaps, on their part that this son, grown to be a man, fifty-seven years later, should dare to carry the knowledge of the religion of Christ across the wide Atlantic, and, for his first act, plant the cross on the shore of the New World.   The pictures of St. Christopher, which one so often sees, represent the saint as bearing the Infant Jesus on his shoulders through a raging river torrent, but Cristoforo Colombo carried the news of the Saviour across three thousand miles of stormy seas to the Land of Promise, which so many of his fellow-countrymen are to-day seeking for their new home.

It would seem that Italy should have profited more by the discoveries of her own Columbus than any other nation, but as a matter of fact, Spain, whose adventurous monarchs had the faith and courage to send him out on his quest for a new world, as well as Portugal and England, profited far more by his discoveries than did Italy. Genoa and Florence lost the control of the Mediterranean, and, singularly enough, it is said that Italy's sea power began to decline from this very year of Columbus' discovery.

Two hundred years of disastrous wars followed the memorable date of 1492. Many powers attempted to get their slice of fair Italy and some succeeded, but the conquerors were often in their turn conquered, and had to give back the cities which they had won with blood and rapine.

In the latter part of the eighteenth century and the early years of the nineteenth that brilliant meteor named Napoleon Buonaparte flashed across the political skies of Europe. Every country felt his heavy hand, and many, like Italy, had reason to bless him for the new era which he introduced. He defeated the Austrians in battle after battle, drove them out of Lombardy and much of northern Italy, and said to his soldiers in a proclamation by no means devoid of truth, "To you will belong the glory of replacing the statues of heroes who have rendered Rome immortal and of rousing the Romans who have become enslaved."

The Italian republicans greatly rejoiced at the advent of Napoleon, and he was soon able to create a Republic, which included Bologna, Ferrara, Ravenna, Reggio and Rodena. The capital of this short-lived state was Bologna. A little later this republic was combined with the Cisalpine republic, including much of the Papal States, Lombardy and Venetia, and Milan became the capital of this new republic.

Pope Pius sided with the Austrians, and Napoleon, punishing him for his partisanship and his treachery, for he had before promised to support the Napoleonic régime, compelled him to give up other cities, in addition to those he had already lost. On Nov. 27, 1798, the great Emperor entered Rome in triumph, and "proclaimed the Tiberine Republic, announcing that the temporal power of the Pope had fallen. Pope Pius VI was seized, the Vatican plundered and its art

treasures sent to Paris.   The Pope was exiled to
France, where he died at Valence in 1799."

About this time, however, Napoleon found
other work as an empire builder and destroyer
in the near East, and sailed for Egypt and Syria,
to renew his conquests on African and Asiatic
soil.   Seeing their great opponent safely off for
Egypt, England, Austria, Russia, Turkey and
Naples joined together in another coalition, and
at first apparently were successful in destroying
the French power in Italy and the republics that
Napoleon had so recently set up were overthrown.

But the triumph of the allies was short-lived.
The only ally which alone the French needed to
turn defeat into victory was the commanding
genius of their great general.   Against this for
many years all the other powers of Europe could
make little headway.   On Oct. 9, 1799, Napoleon returned from Egypt.   Exactly a month
later he overthrew the Directory which he had
left in charge of affairs in Paris.   Eighteen days
later he proclaimed himself the First Consul, and
soon he began his campaign to re-conquer Italy.
His passage over the Great St. Bernard is one
of the most memorable and romantic events in
all history, but it was finally accomplished suc-
cessfully, though with incredible pains and suffering on the part of the soldiers.

The decisive battle of Marengo followed, when the Austrians were driven out of Italy. Once more Italy became a republic and Napoleon made himself her president. The lightning-like, kaleidoscopic changes in Napoleon's career followed rapidly. The First Consul became the Emperor. The Italian Republic became a monarchy, and on May 26, 1805, in the cathedral of Monza, near Milan, he took the crown of Lombardy and placed it upon his own brow, saying, "It is from God; a curse on him who touches it!"

The pretence of a republican government for Italy was now at an end and the peninsula had the same government as France. But the rest of Europe could not allow the usurper from Corsica to enjoy his triumph in peace, and soon another coalition was formed, and an enormous Austrian army was almost annihilated by Napoleon in the Battle of Austerlitz in the last month of 1805. This brought the whole of Venetia, together with the rest of Italy, under Napoleon's sway. A little later he made his brother Joseph king of Italy, and when he transferred him, like a pawn on a chess board to the Iberian Peninsula making him king of Spain, he made Murat, his brother-in-law, king of Naples, and at the same time annexed the rock-ribbed Island of Capri to

Naples, since he had just captured it from the British admiral.

Pius VII had now become Pope, and wished to have his temporal power restored. This Napoleon refused to do, whereupon the Pope excommunicated him. King Murat captured the Pope and imprisoned him in the Palace of Fontainebleau where he languished for five years. Then Buonaparte still further cut up Italy into sections, and, with no fear of nepotism before his eyes, made his sister Eliza the Grand Duchess of Tuscany.

Nevertheless Napoleon's rule was, on the whole, beneficial to Italy. Augusta Hale Gifford, in her "Story of Italy," well says, "His governments were carried on according to the demands of justice, and besides revising the barbarous laws, he made new ones so perfect that they still continue to be used in jurisprudence. It was at this era that the idea of a United Italy was first infused into the hearts of the people. . . . He constructed new roads, and engineered important systems of canals, beside beautifying cities and encouraging the population of the country districts to engage in agricultural pursuits. Napoleon also commenced the renovation of Rome. The ruins of 1800 years in the Forum and on the Palatine were soon excavated and the imposing columns of the temples, and wonderful old palaces were restored in their original grace and stateliness."

CHAPTER III

ITALY IN MODERN TIMES

The downfall of Napoleon plunged Italy into political chaos for many a long year. The troops of the Allies entered Paris in 1814 and the next year, at the Congress of Vienna, they parcelled out the provinces of poor Italy among the most rapacious and persistent of her claimants. Tuscany was given to Ferdinand, the brother of Austria's Emperor. A long, narrow, irregular section extending from Modena on the north to a point half way between Rome and Naples in the south, was given to the Pope. This great section of the most fertile part of Italy contained three millions of people, and supported a standing army of 16,000 men to guard His Holiness Pope Pius VII, who had been liberated after his five years' imprisonment by Napoleon and had returned to Rome.

Marie Louise, Napoleon's second wife, who had not followed him to St. Helena, was made the Duchess of Parma, and was given a very considerable slice of Italian soil in the north.

King Ferdinand I, one of the unspeakable Bourbon dynasty, was again made king of the Two Sicilies, which included Naples, Southern Italy and the island of Sicily.

Thus was Italy again carved up, as of late years the Great Powers have been dividing Africa among themselves, and as they would perhaps have divided China, had not Secretary Hay's policy of the Open Door, and some other obstacles, stood in their way.

The only little strip of Italian soil, which the Allies spared and allowed to maintain independence and self-government, was the minute Republic of San Marino. This tiny Republic, holding bravely to its individuality for fifteen hundred years, amid all the turmoils of war and revolution that have raged around it, appeals to the imagination of every true democrat. St. Marinus, who is said to have been a stone mason, afterwards raised to the rank of saint-hood, by the Pope, fled, it is claimed, from the persecutions of Diocletian with a few comrades, and founded this little state in the wilderness, a state which has never known a king, and whose people still govern themselves, and make their own laws. Doubtless its insignificance has been its chief protection. As even a crowd of bullies would hesitate to abuse a child or rob an infant, so the political bullies and tyrants who ruled Italy for a thousand years left this little state unmolested.

Though the work of Napoleon seemed to have been wholly undone, his plan of a United Italy flouted, and his victories turned into defeat, nevertheless the leaven, which he cast into the meal, never ceased to work, and, though the day was long delayed, and the reactionary forces seemed to be supreme, the glad year of 1848, the year of Europe's awakening, at last dawned, and after twenty-two years more of struggle and defeat and victory, United Italy became no longer an iridescent dream, but an actual fact.

It is interesting to note that even after Napoleon was banished to Elba, during those memorable ninety days, he was urged by the people of Turin to become their leader, with the hope that he might afterwards become the king of United Italy.

I cannot tell at length the stories of the revolutions of 1821 and 1830, for they were soon dwarfed by the greater uprising of 1848, and are chiefly interesting as showing the ferment which was always at work in the Italian character, and the ideals which were never satisfied until Italy was free and united once more.

The year 1848, was indeed a great year for all Europe. In it freedom may be said to have been re-born. In France, in Germany, in Switzerland, the people began to realize that their hour to rule had come, that kings and princes were their servants and not their tyrants. Even in Austria, the most hidebound and reactionary of all European states, the people compelled the Emperor to grant a constitution.

It could not be expected that Italy, where the seed of revolution had been longest planted and the longing for freedom was most intense, would be slow to join in this general awakening of the nations, and indeed it was here that the new ideas received their largest and best development. Some great names, which Italy will never willingly let die, were now engraved upon the scroll of her history.

Charles Albert, the great grandfather of the present monarch, was the king of Savoy and Piedmont. He was a true patriot, and devoted to his country and the cause of her freedom, but he had been considered too cautious if not timid by the more fiery spirits of the revolution, yet he now declared that the hour had struck. He adopted Cavour's sentiment that "doubt, hesitation and delay are no longer possible," and resolved that he would throw himself heart and soul into the fight for a United Italy.

But he was not destined to live to see the desire

of his heart. Like Moses, he could not enter
the Promised Land, though he led his people up
to its very gates. He was defeated by the Austrians, was looked upon with suspicion even by
his own people, because of these disasters, abdi-
cated in favor of his son Victor Emanuel II, and
retired brokenhearted to Spain, where he died a
few months later.

His greatest triumph, as is the case with so
many other true men, came after his death. It
has been well said that when his body was
brought back for burial to his own beloved land,
"Italy recognized his sterling virtues and made
him her patron saint. Bands of pilgrims journeyed to his tomb, and from that time, all felt
that to do honor to his memory, they must serve
Italy."

But Charles Albert, though wise and patriotic,
and the nominal ruler during the early days of
the struggle for liberty, was not the chief hero,
certainly not the only hero, of the new order.
He must at least divide his honors with three
remarkable men who were as providentially
raised up to secure Italian liberty and unity, as
were Washington and Franklin and Jefferson to
secure the liberty of our own republic. Whether
great times produce great men, or great men
usher in great days may be a mooted question,

but certain it is that when they were needed most, Mazzini, Cavour and Garibaldi came to the front as the saviors of Italy. Miss Gifford, in her "History of Italy," has thus wisely written of these men:

"Of the three leaders, Mazzini was said to be the prophet, Cavour the statesman, and Garibaldi the knight errant of Italian independence. They were all natives of the Sardinian kingdom, Mazzini from Genoa, Garibaldi from Nice, and Cavour from Piedmont. . . . Cavour had the genius of the statesman, together with practical sense and great swiftness of detail; and, though, but for the others he could not have been the savior of Italy, without him Mazzini's fanatical effort would have been abortive, and Garibaldi's dexterous strokes in arms must have resulted in failure."

Doubtless Cavour was the greatest of these Three Mighty Men, and though there were many others who coöperated with them, men of undoubted wisdom and of no mean ability, yet, as when David's heroes were enumerated, "There were none others that attained unto the first three." Mazzini's fiery eloquence aroused the people, but he was by no means well balanced, nor was he patient and wise enough to deliver the people from their bondage. Garibaldi was a brilliant general, strategist and fighter. He was the fascinating Phil Sheridan of his day, but Cavour was the Lincoln of the revolution, wise, statesmanlike, patient, undismayed, and to him the young king, Victor Emanuel II, wisely confided the direction of the affairs of the state, acknowledging his superior wisdom in the halls of council, while he with fiery intrepidity led the forces on the field of battle.

Garibaldi is the best known of the trio in our own country, for he spent five years of his exile in the United States, and probably no foreigner, unless it be Kossuth, was ever received with such unbounded enthusiasm by the American people. As in the case of Kossuth, articles of wearing apparel were called by Garibaldi's name, and he has been enshrined in our Valhalla, with heroes who fought our own battles and won our own liberties.

We must dismiss the story of these gallant years in a few sentences, but it must not be supposed that freedom and unity were won in any brief campaign. Victory followed defeat, and a new defeat came hard on the heels of victory. For many years the liberty and the unity of Italy hung in the balance.

In the Crimean War, Italy sided with England and France against Russia, for Cavour felt that Russian despotism ill accorded with Italy's desire for freedom, and that she must range herself side by side with the enlightened forces of constitutional government. Afterwards he persuaded Napoleon III, who had now come to the throne of France, to side with Italy against Austria, and after the battle of Magenta, which resulted in an overwhelming victory for the French and Italians, the two kings, Victor Emanuel and Napoleon, entered Milan in triumph.

The bloody battle of Solferino followed in a few days, and in these two terrible struggles it is said that more than sixty thousand men were killed and wounded. Such was a part of the price in human blood that Italy paid for her freedom.

Francis Joseph had then come to the throne of Austria, and, indeed, was in command of the Austrian army at the battle of Solferino. As we review the stirring momentous years which have elapsed between 1848 and the present, years that have meant so much, not only to Italy, but to all the world, it is difficult to realize that the young monarch who assumed the throne of Austria in 1848, the revolutionary year, was nearly seventy years later the venerable Emperor of the Austrians who died only a short time before his own country went down to ignominious defeat.

In 1859, after the battle of Solferino, it seemed as though Austria's power was forever broken, but Louis Napoleon earned his title of Turn-coat, by making peace with Francis Joseph at Villafranca, without consulting Victor Emanuel, and only a part of the fruit of victory which Italy should have received, became hers. Moreover, Napoleon now claimed Savoy and Nice as a reward for his alliance with Italy, and though to give up Savoy was for Victor Emanuel, the King of Savoy, to renounce "the cradle of his monarchy," Italy was not strong enough to resist the demands, and from that day to this Savoy and Nice have belonged to France.

During the next ten years war followed war, and the soil of Italy was often stained with patriot blood, but at last Austria was obliged to give up Venetia to Napoleon III, who shortly handed it over to Victor Emanuel, greatly to the joy of the Venetians, who rapturously greeted the Italian King, when he entered Venice as its ruler, on November 7, 1866.

The conquest of Rome by the Italian patriots was now all that was wanting to secure the unity of Italy, but Rome for many years had been defended and the Pope kept securely in his place by French soldiers, and as France had been the chief ally of Italy, there seemed to be no way of dislodging him. However, Providence opened the way in 1870. When Napoleon began his disastrous war with Prussia, every French soldier was needed in the fight against this mighty foe, so his troops were withdrawn from Rome after seventeen years of French rule, and the Pope had to look out for himself.

When the French were finally defeated at Sedan, and the Republic of France was proclaimed, there were no obstacles to the entrance of the Italian troops. Victor Emanuel, desiring a peaceful occupation, earnestly urged Pius IX, who was then Pope, to give up his temporal power, saying that "he regarded his spiritual office with the profoundest reverence, but that the exigencies of the times demanded the downfall of his temporal power, and it was hoped that he would yield amicably."

This the Pope absolutely refused to do, and commanded that "there should be only a sufficient exhibition of force to prove to the world that his realms were taken away from him by military violence."

The twentieth of September, 1870, was indeed a glad day for Italy. No wonder that there is a "Twentieth of September" street in every considerable Italian city. On that day, at half past nine o'clock in the morning, the *Porta Pia* was battered down, and through this demolished gateway the soldiers of United Italy entered the Eternal City. The Pope shut himself up in the Vatican, claiming that 'he was a prisoner, and for nearly fifty years his successors have maintained the same figment. Nevertheless, the Italian troops have dealt most kindly and generously with him. A regiment of Italian troops was at once stationed in the Vatican Gardens to protect Pius IX. An annual allowance of nearly a million dollars has been granted to the Pope by the Italian government, an allowance which it is said the Popes have always refused to touch, lest they should seem to acquiesce in the claims of the government.

Rome was soon made the capital of United Italy. The great result for which patriots had been longing and praying and fighting for nearly a hundred years had been accomplished and Victor Emanuel could say: "My heart thrills as I salute all the representatives of our united country for the first time, and say, Italy is free and united; it only remains for us to make her great, prosperous and happy."

CHAPTER IV

ITALY TO-DAY

"Now that Italy is made, we must make the Italians!" exclaimed an Italian statesman named Massino d'Azeglio, something more than fifty years ago. To the making of Italians as well as of Italy, have the years since the entry of Victor Emanuel's troops into Rome been largely devoted. Until Italy's entrance into the European war, they were for the most part years of external peace and of internal development.

It is true that their peaceful history was marred by two wars, one the disastrous Abyssinian War from which Italy had to retire so ingloriously, a war which only added increased taxation and neither glory, territory, nor spoil, to the already overburdened nation; the other was the more successful, but scarcely more justifiable war in Tripoli, which added large domains and large responsibilities to the kingdom, and affords an outlet to her surplus population, of which, as yet, she has taken little advantage.

During all these later years Italy has been

On the Roman Campagna

blessed with wise and conscientious monarchs,
who have sought to reign rather than to rule,
and for the most part the affairs of state have
been managed by able politicians, many of whom
have been of the calibre and rank of statesmen.
Of Victor Emanuel II, the dashing soldier and
intrepid general, we have already spoken. He
was a true patriot, and subordinated his own interests to the good of the nation. In this respect
how different is his story and that of his successors from that of many of his early predecessors, the emperors of Rome, whose profligacy,
debauchery, corruption and cruelty have made
their names malodorous on the pages of ancient
history.

Victor Emanuel's purpose and character are
indicated by his address from the throne at the
opening of the first parliament, in which he said,
"The work to which we have consecrated our
lives is completed. Italy is restored after long
and sacrificing effort. Everything speaks to us
not only of past greatness but of future duties,
and in the joy of the occasion we must not forget
our responsibilities. Regenerated by liberty,
may we seek in freedom and order the secret of
strength, and endeavor to reconcile church and
state."

This last endeavor was indeed a difficult one,

not because of lack of sincere desire and effort on the part of the king and his ministers, but because of the attitude of the Pope and the ecclesiastics.   Pius IX had begun his career with liberal views, and had contributed not a little to the realization of a free and united Italy.   However when it came to giving up every vestige of his temporal power, he became a reactionary and even refused to receive the messengers of Victor Emanuel II whom he sent to the Pope, when the king took up his residence at the Quirinal, to declare his personal allegiance to the Church and to congratulate Pius IX on so long occupying the Pontifical Chair.

The disdain with which this messenger, and others who came on a similar errand, were received at the Vatican, widened the breach between church and state.   The Pope forbade his followers to vote in the elections, or to have anything to do with the new government.   As a result the people of Rome who voted were absolutely unanimous when they renounced all allegiance to the Pope as a temporal ruler, and acknowledged, in affairs of state, their fealty to the King alone.   Of course the vote would have been far from unanimous if the clerical party had voted, but they declared that they were "overawed by 60,000 bayonets and that any appeal to the ballot box was a farce."

This stand-off attitude toward civic affairs has been maintained by the successors of Pius IX, who still keep up the fiction that they are prisoners in the Vatican, but, as a recent writer has said, "If the Vatican is a prison, the door is locked from the inside, and the Pope keeps the the key. It is a very luxurious prison, with its 11,000 rooms, its museums, its libraries, and galleries with their priceless treasures, and with expensive gardens and grounds. It is a palace of delights. . . . The Pope had his little army of some 600 gaily dressed Swiss; he has his private post and telegraph arrangements; he has his ambassadors accredited to him from foreign Catholic powers, and he has—the Vatican."

Of late years, since the genii of socialism have escaped from the bottle in which they were so long corked up, and have spread throughout Italy in such a threatening cloud, the *non expedit* laws which issued from the Vatican have been somewhat modified, and to defeat syndicalism and the more violent forms of socialism, Catholics have been allowed to vote, and Catholic nobles have vigorously electioneered.

Pius IX was succeeded by the astute and

learned Leo XIII, considered by his enemies a wily intriguer, and by his friends a brilliant statesman, who, though he was 68 years old when he was crowned with the triple crown of the Pope, exercised his office far longer than most of his predecessors.

He in turn was followed by the gentle ecclesiastic whose name "Pius" was acknowledged by all to indicate his character. He was a devout, godly man undoubtedly, but narrow and intensely reactionary in his theological views, who did his utmost to destroy Modernism in the Church, but who maintained an increasingly friendly attitude toward the civil rulers of Italy. In spite of the "Prisoner-of-the-Vatican" fiction, which he seemed to feel it necessary to maintain, he and his advisers seemed to accept the fact that the temporal power of the papacy was forever at an end.

The character and policy of the present Pope Benedict are too little known to allow characterization here, but he is considered, by those who know him, to be a wise and friendly ecclesiastic, whose efforts for peace have shown a kindly heart, though the exigencies of the world war made those efforts fruitless, and sometimes laid him open to the charge of pro-Germanism by the Allies.

To return to Victor Emanuel—he reigned wisely and well for nearly thirty years as a strictly constitutional monarch, "preserving amidst the splendors of a great court the simple tastes of his early life." He died at Rome of a fever on the 9th of January, 1878, and was buried in the Pantheon. The open dome lets in the light and air of heaven upon his magnificent tomb.

Here, beside Raphael and other distinguished Italians, he rests in his long, last sleep. His homely, democratic ways, which so endeared him to his people, will long be remembered. A well-known writer tells the story of a countryman who was trying to lift his wagon out of the mire, when he saw a strong, burly stranger passing, and said, "I should think you might lend a hand in lifting this wagon." "Certainly," replied the stranger, as he put his shoulder to the wheel and lifted the vehicle on to level ground. At this moment a traveller coming along made a humble obeisance, and the rustic, greatly humiliated, discovered that his friend in need had been the king of Italy.

King Victor's son and successor, Humbert I, carried out the wise, progressive, democratic policy of his father, and when, after a reign of some twenty-two years, he was assassinated by the anarchist, Angelo Bresci, the grief of the people over his violent and untimely end was scarcely less than that exhibited at the death of his father.

The present King succeeded Humbert I with the title Victor Emanuel III, and so far has proved worthy of the noble ancestors who bore it before him. He was born in 1869, and, as Prince of Naples before his father's death, for many years held his court in that immense red palace which is so familiar to the thousands of American travellers who have sailed through the blue Gulf of Naples, into the harbor of that commanding and picturesque city.

It seemed strange to many that the Prince of Naples should seek a wife in the little principality of Montenegro, and should go over the forbidding Black Mountains to the provincial capital of Cettinje, which is hardly larger than an American village, to find a bride. Any one who has climbed the interminable zigzags which lead over the precipitous mountains from Cattaro on the Dalmatian coast to the sparsely settled Montenegrin territory, which for the most part is wild, forbidding and desolate in the extreme, would consider it the last place to which the prospective monarch of a great country would go to seek a wife. However this was a love match. Prince

Victor Emanuel and Princess Heléne did not meet first in Cettinje, but in Venice, at the Exhibition of Fine Arts, and he could scarcely have chosen one better fitted to be the Queen of Italy.

Her common sense and kindness have endeared her to her people, as the same qualities have made her husband popular with all classes. The following story is told of the Queen as illustrating her goodness of heart and her spirit of courtesy. It is said that at one time some ladies called upon her when she was busy with her children, and she was obliged to keep them waiting a little while. When she at last received them, she apologized courteously for the delay, and was afterwards taken to task by some of her advisers, who told her that it was not for her to apologize; she must not forget that she was the Queen. To which she replied, "Yes, but I do not wish to forget that before I was a queen I was a lady." It is this spirit of courteous kindness that has greatly helped to endear her to her people.

Having told briefly the story of the kings and popes, what can we say of the progress of the common people, since Italy became a free and united nation? It is largely the purpose of the rest of this book to tell their story, to show how they live, what advances they have made, what obstacles in their upward march they have met, what leaders in literature, art and science they look up to, why so many of them seek a new home in our own land, and what qualities of brain and brawn they bring with them to America.

It must not be forgotten, as has been said before, that Italy is practically a young nation, born indeed many centuries ago, but reborn within the lifetime of men who are now only in middle age. Those who do not yet consider themselves old, heard the triumphal shouts on the twentieth of September, 1870, when the breach was made in the Porta Pia, and the army of United Italy entered the Eternal City. The contemporaries of Cavour, Mazzini and Garibaldi are still living, and some of them are prominent leaders in Italian politics to-day.

It is not fair to compare the progress of a country so young in its national life with a country like Great Britain, which has enjoyed centuries of stable government and constitutional liberty, or even with a country like our own which, in addition to unbounded natural resources, has for nearly a century and a half had a comparatively pure national government, and an uninterrupted succession of patriotic and conscientious presidents.

When we remember the practical youth of Italy as a nation, when we recall the tremendous burdens imposed by the former régime in the shape of high taxes, illiteracy and constant struggles with the dominant church, it seems wonderful that the kingdom has made such rapid and substantial progress. Cities like Rome have been practically rebuilt. Miles of slums, as in Naples, have been abolished, though there are other miles waiting the destructive hand of enlightened progress. Tunnels have pierced the Alps. Railroads have gridironed the country, north and east and south and west. Tens of thousands of schools have been established. The suffrage has been extended, until now, perhaps, it is as nearly universal as in most democratic countries. Marshes which have bred malaria for thousands of years have been drained. Canals have been dug and aqueducts built at tremendous cost.

Together with this material advance the intellectual progress of the nation has kept pace with these more tangible forms of growth. Arts and letters have flourished. In some lines of science and invention Italy has led the way. Still much, very much remains to be done before Italy can fully take the place to which she is apparently destined by Providence. What has been accomplished, and what remains yet to be done for the people, what they are to-day, and what they may become in their own land, or in the newer Italy across the sea, what effect the world war may have on Italy's fortunes; these matters must be the subjects of succeeding chapters.

CHAPTER V

What about the common people? How has
the overthrow of the Bourbons, and the expul-
sion of the Austrians, and the abolition of the
temporal power of the Pope, affected the mass
of the people? Has free Italy made a free people? Has united Italy united the sons of the soil
and the workshop for their own betterment and
uplift? In a large and general way these ques-
tions must be answered in the affirmative. It is
true that there are problems yet to be solved, and
Italy has yet leagues and leagues to go, before
she reaches the goal which her best patriots have
in view. Nevertheless when we consider the vast
progress which has already been made, when we
remember that New Italy is not yet half a century old, when we remember the Hills Difficult
which have already been surmounted, and the
Slough of Despond out of which she has emerged,
we can believe that nothing is impossible, and
that Italy may yet take her assured place in the
forefront of the civilized nations of the world.

All these conditions and changes for the better have a distinct and important bearing upon the American of the future. I do not believe that the tide of emigration from Italy to the United States will slacken for many a decade to come, except temporarily after the world war, and everything that is done to purify the fountain at its source will purify the stream that will pour with constantly increasing volume into America. It is cheering, then, to turn for a little to the remarkable social and industrial progress which Italy has made since, defeated and broken-hearted, the great grandfather of the present king renounced his royal throne and fled as an exile to Spain.

To begin with the soil, the basis of all wealth and industry. Writing a few years ago, Bolton King and Thomas Okey in their "Italy of To-Day" said:

"It may seem extravagant to talk of a revival in the present pass of Italian agriculture. When the income of a poor farmer or regular laborer's family seldom ranges beyond twenty-five pounds a year, when the exhausted land produces less than half a crop of wheat; when, through large districts, the barest elements of modern agriculture are unknown, when a vicious land-system and dearth of capital half strangle progress, it

is hard at first to believe that there is any dawn of
better things.   And yet there is a revival almost
as notable as that which has awakened the country's industry to new life.   Emigration and the
increasing intercourse with the towns, have
broken up the old benumbing apathy of the peasant.   His standard of comfort has arisen; his
clothes and furniture are better; shoes are worn
by all, where shoes were unknown forty years
ago; the women wear hats and earrings, and ape
the fashions of the town; tobacco takes the place
of snuff, and almost every peasant has his occa-
sional luxury at the café or tavern.   Methods of
agriculture steadily improve.   Even at the time
of the *Inchiesta agraria* the improved stock and
implements, the better rotation of crops, the increased use of manure, were making themselves
felt, and since then the advance has been much
more rapid."

The improvements of which these authors
write have been gathering momentum during the
last few years, and the picture could now be
painted in much brighter colors.

And yet, as the observant traveller gazes out
of the car window, or drives through the fragrant lanes in the early days of the lovely Italian spring, he need not be an agricultural expert
to see that the laborers on the soil still literally

have a hard row to hoe.   In many parts of Italy
he will see comparatively few horses pulling plow
or harrow, but often great, white, wide-horned
oxen, sometimes four pairs hitched to a plow, and
he will compare their slow and toilsome progress
through the furrow with the steam plows of our
own prairies, that throw up a score of furrows at
a time, and break up fifty acres in a day.   More
often, perhaps, he will see a row of laborers, men
and women alike, in a long line, with pointed,
heart-shaped spades, toilsomely digging up the
soil by hand, and, when he remembers the pitiable pay which this back-breaking work brings in,
he will perhaps come to the conclusion that, after
all, little progress has been made, and that the lot
of the Italian agricultural laborer is the most un-
enviable of all.

But progress is shown not by the actual position where one finds himself, but by the distance
he has come.   We must look not at the present
only, but at the past, to see whether the laborer
is on the up-hill road, and this view leaves no
doubt that he is facing upward as well as plodding onward.   The old rhyme, written doubtless
by some English aristocrat, in order to make his
tenants contented with their lot, ran as follows:

"Honest John Tomkins, the hedger and ditcher,
Though he always was poor, never wished to be richer."

This rhyme is certainly not true of the Italian laborer. Before the era of United Italy he was little better than a serf, and such is his condition in some parts of Sicily to-day, but for the most part, he is no longer the man with the muck-rake, but has seen the crown of prosperity and progress above his head, even though he has not yet been able fully to grasp it.

One long step in advance has been taken in making agriculture a comparatively healthy and safe pursuit. What life could be more free from disease and danger, my reader will ask, than that of the farmer? But it was not so a few years ago in Italy. In many parts the ploughed field was then as dangerous as a battlefield. A dozen years since a careful author wrote, "Malaria slays its twenty thousand victims every year, and keeps desolate huge tracts of the richest land in Italy." But about that time, it was discovered that the pestiferous mosquito was alone responsible for spreading malaria.

In the worst parts of the Campagna it was found by intrepid experimenters that one could live and thrive in a mosquito-proof hut. Since then this scourge of the Campagna and of many other parts of Italy, has been largely conquered, and it is at least as safe to belong to the army of agricultural laborers, as to be even in peace times in the army of King Emanuel III. The same wonderful discovery that made it possible to dig the Panama Canal, has made the low lands of Italy comparatively safe. The mosquito that dismayed and conquered De Lesseps has in its turn been conquered by scientists. Millions of acres have consequently been reclaimed from the marshes, and are now rejoicing in the olive, orange and fig as in the palmiest days of Rome.

When we think how the Campagna of Rome two thousand years ago was a garden spot of the world, how it was covered with beautiful villas, was fragrant with flowers, shaded with umbrageous trees, and filled with vineyards and orange groves, how it produced the finest fruits and vegetables; when we remember how, for hundreds of years past, it has been almost as uninhabitable as the desert of Sahara, we can see what remains to be done, and understand some of the possibilities of Italian agriculture.

Other great districts containing millions of acres can be made fruitful by irrigation, and the re-foresting of the hillsides will prevent the disastrous floods which have destroyed the industry of other parts of Italy.

Another peculiar danger of Italian agriculture, in which many countries do not share, is the hail storm, and we are told that the Hail Insurance Societies have charged as high as five dollars per acre to insure the vineyards against disaster from this source. It would seem as though this were a visitation from heaven, and could not be guarded against by the skill of man, but the authorities I have already quoted tell us that within the last few years experiments of discharging cannon loaded with a special pyrite powder at an advancing hail cloud have been extensively practised in northern Italy, and with satisfactory results. "Whatever may be the scientific explanation, it seems fairly well established that the discharge almost invariably brings down the hail in the form of fine snow. It has been proposed to make the establishment of stations of these *cannoni grandinifugi* compulsory."

The progress of manufactures has been much more marked than the progress of agriculture, particularly in the north, where the high duties imposed by the government on all manufactured goods imported from abroad have protected, to an unreasonable extent, as many think, the products of the factories, the rolling mills and the machine shops of Turin and Milan and other cities of northern Italy. The complaints of the south against being taxed for the benefit of the north have been long and loud, and the government has now made concessions in the way of reduced taxation on manufacturing plants to Naples and that vicinity which have in some degree allayed the clamor.

But all this improvement in agriculture and the mechanic arts would hardly make a people great and prosperous unless education went hand in hand with material improvement. In this respect, too, Italy has made strides with seven-league boots, though she has not as yet by any means caught up with the most advanced countries. Still she had a long way to go, since, before the days of United Italy, sixty, eighty and, in some sections, ninety per cent of the people were illiterate. In the Papal States and in southern Italy it was the exceptional man who could read or write. Now, take it the country over, only forty per cent of the people are illiterate, even including the most benighted parts of Italy, while in some sections, as in Turin, there is practically no illiteracy.

Formerly the schools were all under the control of the priests. Poor and inadequate they were indeed, except for a few of the wealthy classes. Now, education is a matter of national concern, and excellent laws for compulsory schooling, up to the age of fourteen, have been passed. If the resources of the country were equal to the intentions of the rulers, there would

soon be no child in Italy who did not know at least
his three R's.   But, alas, many parts of Italy are
still desperately poor.   The immense appropria-
tions for the army and navy, which the Italians
have thought necessary to sustain their national
dignity even before the recent war, left comparatively little in the national treasury for education, and many rural communities are absolutely too poverty-stricken to afford a decent
school.   Universal disarmament, even if partial,
would greatly advance Italian education.

Of late years, however, the smaller communities have been combining their resources, thus
obtaining better schools and better teachers, and
the idea of Universal Education is constantly being approached, though it still seems to beckon
from afar.

As to religious education, ethics and morals are
taught in the government schools, but religion is
left to the ecclesiastical authorities, who, however, have free access to the schools, to teach their
dogmas at certain hours, an instruction which, I
understand, is given gratuitously.

When one sees the crowd of ragamuffins that
swarm in every street and alley of Naples and
some other cities of the south, at every hour of
the day and night, one is tempted to wonder if
compulsory education is not, after all, a farce.

140523

Undoubtedly it is in many sections, but when in other cities one sees crowds of rosy-faced children, many of them patched but clean, going to, or returning from, school, with their slates and their satchels of books, one realizes the progress which a half century has made, and also the further fact that Italy, though united, is not yet homogeneous, and that what is true of one part of the peninsula may be utterly untrue of another part.   The man who has studied only the south is ill-prepared to write about the north, and *vice versa*.

Nevertheless the same leaven is working in all parts of the kingdom, and some day the sunny south will doubtless catch up, in the matter of education, with the more progressive north.   It is even now true that any child in Italy, who really desires an education, and is willing to work out his sums like Abraham Lincoln, by the light of a fire, and on the back of a shovel, need not grow up without at least the rudiments of an education.

CHAPTER VI

In considering the qualities of a nation that had long been sending a third of a million of its people to our shores every year before the world war began, it is of even more importance to consider their ideals and aspirations, their general trend of character, than to know their history and their actual achievements. Crossing the Atlantic will not alter the character of a people. The salt sea breezes will not blow away their ideals. It may fairly be said that the ideals of the Italians are not only unity and freedom and progress, as we have already seen from their history, but democracy and coöperation for a better social state.

Of course I do not mean to say that every poor Italian emigrant consciously cherishes these ideals; he may theoretically scarcely know the difference between a democracy and a monarchy, and he may never have reasoned about "social uplift," but, nevertheless, the desire for these things is in his blood, and under favorable cir-

53

cumstances will assert itself. The peasants responded as readily as the upper classes to the fiery eloquence of Mazzini, to the bold leadership of Garibaldi, and, so far as they had a voice, supported the wise efforts for freedom and unity of Cavour.

It is true that republicanism, as a cult, has a very slight hold on the Italians. They are satisfied with their king and his court, even though they may growl at the nearly a million dollars a year which is given to him as an allowance. But they approve of the monarchy, mainly because it is, so to speak, a republican monarchy. It is inconceivable that a Bomba, as Ferdinand I was called, because he was said to rule his people with explosive bombs, could ever again sit on the throne of Naples. The democratic, simple, homely ways of their kings, since New Italy was born, have always commended them to their people, and even the passing traveller notices the self-respecting, independent, though not ungenial, air of the average Italian. There is nothing of cringing servility about him. He does not seem ready to lick your boots for a penny, as do some of the lower classes in Europe. In many an English shop, if you make a small purchase, the obsequious merchant will say, "Thank you, thank you, thank you," a dozen times before you can get out of the door. It is impossible that any man should feel as grateful to you for spending a sixpence as such words indicate, and you at once doubt his sincerity as well as resent his manner.

The Italian peasant will greet you politely, but without any shade of servility, as though he, too, were a man and a brother.

Alas, on our side of the water, in the second generation, this independence may degenerate into impudence, but it is at least more in accordance with American ideals than a toad-eating habit that worships a lord or a bishop.

This democratic spirit has been fostered by the privileges of the suffrage, which is as nearly universal in Italy as in any modern country. Property tests and educational tests have been practically done away with, and any citizen over twenty-one years of age can vote. It is true that if he is under thirty years of age, and has not served in the army, he cannot vote unless he can read and write, but there are so few who come under this category that they hardly make an exception to the rule of universal suffrage.

Women have not yet attained the right of the ballot, and this is true of every other European country except Finland, Great Britain, and Germany, but it would not be strange if Italy should be the next large nation to bestow the ballot upon her daughters.   There are two strong Woman's Suffrage organizations in Italy, which have not adopted militant tactics but which, on this account, are all the more effective, and likely soon to succeed.

One of these parties is composed of devout Catholic women who are eager for the suffrage as soon as the Holy Father of the Vatican gives his consent.   The other party demands it with or without the pontifical blessing, and I am told they are making rapid headway in their propaganda. As soon as they convince the majority of the Italian people that woman's suffrage is wise and necessary, they will doubtless gain their end, for in these days the Italians have a way of securing what they set their hearts upon.

It must be admitted that the evils often connected with universal suffrage are not unknown in Italy, and at times bribery and corruption have been unblushing and almost unrebuked.   In the general election of 1909, we are told, the charge of wholesale corruption was made "in the chamber, and the evidence given before the elections' commission read like scenes from a comic opera. The absent, the illiterate, the dead, voted in hundreds.   The trick known in Sicily as *fare il coppino,* which consists in thrusting enough forged papers into the ballot boxes before they are sealed to ensure a candidate's return, had been freely practised."

In order to make sure that the goods are delivered, it is said that the briber is accustomed to give to the bribed one half of a bank note before, and the corresponding half, after the vote has been recorded, and since the Italian voter has to write his name on the ballot, a piece of blotting paper is given him, on which he has to show the impress of the candidate's name, to prove that he has voted for the candidate of the man who has paid him for his ballot.

But let not Americans hold up their hands in holy horror, or at least self-righteous horror, for, alas! repeaters and bribers and ballot-box stuffers have not been unknown on our side of the Atlantic. We can only rejoice that a quickened civic conscience every year makes such corruption more rare and less tolerable, and I am glad to read on the authority of a well-informed writer, that "the scandals of 1909 in Italy invoked a healthy disgust among all shades of opinion, and a genuine desire for drastic remedies."

The power to combine and coöperate for the public good is another sign of a sensible and virile people, and this quality the Italians have in a marked measure. Italian unity could never have been achieved had this not been true. The interests of the north and south, of Sicily and Piedmont, are so diverse in many respects, that only by a willingness to sacrifice something for the general welfare, has the history of the last fifty years been made possible.

The contrast between the federated states of North America and the republics of northern South America, with their constant revolutions and incessant turmoils is largely a matter of racial ability to unite and coöperate for the common good. The United States of North America have been an established and potent factor in the history of the world for more than a hundred years. The United States of South America seems as far from realization as when Pizarro murdered Atahualpa in his palace at Cuzco. In this respect the Italians seem to pattern more nearly after the Anglo-Saxon races than after their brothers of other Latin nations.

This ability to unite their interests has resulted in the multiplication of all kinds of coöperative enterprises. People's banks, savings banks, friendly societies of all sorts flourish in Italy. There are coöperative dairies and bakeries, and agricultural unions and all kinds of union efforts to benefit different classes of the people, which, for the most part, are wisely conceived and ably manned. The dairy business of Italy has been vastly benefited, to mention but one instance, by this ability of the Italians to coöperate, and Italy before the war sent its butter and cheese by parcels' post to distant and less progressive countries, like Spain and Egypt, reaping a large profit thereby.

It is to be expected that among people who have thus learned to combine their efforts, trades unions, or whatever corresponds to them, should be strong. There is probably no city in the world where they have the ability to dictate their own terms as in Rome. The traveller sometimes has occasion to realize this fact to his annoyance and discomfort.

In the first chapter of this book I alluded to a strike which I once witnessed in Rome. For two days the strikers were able absolutely to stop the wheels of industry. No traveller could reach his hotel by bus or tram-car or public carriage. No one could get away if he had heavy baggage to move, for no porters or draymen were on duty. The baker's rolls, which constitute the main portion of the Italian breakfast, were hard and dry and almost uneatable, since, toward the end of the strike, they had been out of the oven for fully three days. The streets were littered with paper and rubbish of every kind, and looked most disreputable, for no street cleaner wielded his broom, or flushed the gutters with the water which is everywhere abundant in Rome. Even the flower sellers on the Spanish Stairs deserted their posts, and no gallant could buy so much as a bunch of violets for his inamorata.

I have never seen such an absolute and effective tie-up of every industry. And what was it all about? Simply because, on account of long-standing abuses, the government had shut up some of the older hospitals of the city, though new and better ones had been provided. The people, however, felt that the action was too drastic and radical; the papers universally opposed the government in the matter, and the strikers had the general sympathy of the public, who were willing to live on dry bread, and walk miles to their destinations, until at last the government gave way and opened the old hospitals once more. Then, as if by magic, the tram wheels began to turn, the drivers of victorias cracked their whips in the same maddening way as of old, the shutters came down from ten thousand little shops, and the normal life of Rome was resumed once more.

It may be said that this is a deadly dangerous state of affairs, when the syndicalists, for a comparatively trivial reason, can thus paralyze the nerve of industry, and by a single edict produce great inconvenience, if not suffering. It must be borne in mind, however, that they only succeed when the people as a whole are with them. Two years before this strike, at the beginning of the Libyan War, a similar strike was ordered by the radical socialists, who did not believe in the war and wished to rebuke the government, but the war was popular, and only the socialists themselves were rebuked, for less than thirty per cent of those who were called out obeyed the demand of the syndicalists, and the wheels of life moved on as usual in Rome. The socialists were laughed at for their pains; it was thought that their power was broken, and they had not dared to call for another universal strike until the one that I have described, in March of 1914. All this only proves that in Italy, as in America, a strike succeeds only when it has the sentiment of the people behind it.

The socialists, though a strong and growing force in Italy, are, as elsewhere, divided into various sections, some being much more radical than others. The anarchistic section, while bold and defiant, is held in check by the larger number of more moderate socialists, and both parties, and all shades of socialism, are consistently and energetically opposed by the Roman Catholic Church, which, in spite of its loss of temporal power, is by no means to be despised as a factor in the politics of Italy.

Another factor of the national life, which tends to make the Italian emigrant a good American citizen, is the lack of centralization in Italy. There is no one overwhelmingly predominant city to absorb the civic pride of the rest of the country. If it is not true, as is sometimes said, that Paris is France, it is very largely true that Buenos Aires is Argentina, and Rio de Janeiro is Brazil. It is true that Sao Paulo is an important center, and in some respects more enterprising and progressive than Rio de Janeiro, but it is also true that the wealth of Brazil is largely centered in its capital, and still more true that the great landed proprietors of Argentina are absentee landlords, and spend their immense wealth in making one gorgeous capital instead of a prosperous and inviting country for the native or the immigrant.

Italy has half a dozen large cities, but no one of supreme importance, and it has a multitude of small towns, each with its noble history, its cherished traditions, its civic pride, which lead its inhabitants proudly to say, "I am from Verona," or "I from Padua," or "I from Parma," or "I from Monza." Such a wide diversity of local interests, such love for and pride in one's home

The Amphitheater at Pompeii

surroundings is a great asset of national character. It is the same quality that makes the resident of the smallest hamlet in Massachusetts, or New York or California or Florida feel that he lives in the best state in the Union, and that the Union is the "best country that the sun ever shone upon." While this sectional pride may foster conceit and bombast in shallow souls, it is at least better than indifference to the claims of one's home and country.

CHAPTER VII

THE INTELLECTUAL LIFE OF MODERN ITALY

In attempting to become better acquainted with the Italian immigrant, it is important to know something of the intellectual life of the country from which he comes. It is true that there are not many poets or painters or sculptors in the steerage accommodations of the Atlantic liners, and few "mute, inglorious Miltons," probably step ashore at Ellis Island. Nevertheless, in this matter, as in all others, the fountain-head affects the stream that flows from it, and, if the Italian nature is of the stuff of which poets and artists are made, we may well believe that some beautiful blossoms will, in time, appear upon the humblest scions of this stock.

We need not go back to ancient times to prove the literary and artistic ability of this branch of the Latin race, for it may be said that since the days of Virgil and Horace, of Salust and Cicero, or even since the times of Dante and Raphael and Michael Angelo, there have been so many changes in the character and ideals of the Italians, and so much new blood has been infused into the body politic that their genius could hardly affect the emigrant of to-day.   So we will confine this chapter to a few brief allusions to the intellectual life in Italy, as manifested in recent years.

Modern Italian literature has been handicapped by more than one weight, and it is the more wonderful that it has made, and is making, for itself a place of no mean importance.   As in our own country, Italy, during the last fifty years, has called for men of action rather than for men of the study and the cloister.   The pick and the shovel, the steam engine and the electric drill have been more in evidence in modern Italy, as in America, than the pen and the artist's brush and palette.

Again, as the authors of "Italy To-Day" assert, "Literary Italian is and always has been a conventional language, nowhere spoken as a living tongue, nowhere a medium for the expression of intimate realities of life.   It, therefore, lacks that vivifying contact with popular sentiment and activity so essential to a great national literature."   I give this opinion for what it is worth, and have little doubt that other authors equally well informed would say that much Italian literature of the last decade or two speaks the living tongue of the living people.   But these authors are undoubtedly correct when they say, "Italians, by the exigencies of their national condition, and by the predominant tone of their minds, have been directed to economic and social studies, rather than to *belles-lettres*. . . . There is an amazing output of economic, social and scientific literature. Many of its exponents are men of European fame: Lombroso in criminology, Grassi in biology, Loria in economics, Villari in history, are but a few."

When we remember that the reading public for pure literature in Italy is as yet comparatively limited, and that few poets or novelists could here live by their pens, the amount of good literature which is produced is the more remarkable. D'Annunzio is perhaps the Italian writer best known outside of Italy. It is unfortnate that this is so, for, as has been said, "his novels are essentially studies in mental and sexual pathology, and there is hardly an important character in them who is a sane, healthy, human being."

We are told that even French translators, when rendering his stories into their own language, have to expurgate some of his viler passages. Unfortunately his example has been followed by some modern English and American authors, who have gone to the very verge of decency, and beyond it, in their realism.

De Amici's vividly picturesque books of travel are known to many American authors, and his stories are equally fascinating, though florid in their style.

Antonio Fogazzaro is thought by many to stand at the head of Italian authors, at least of the writers of fiction, and, unlike D'Annunzio's, his work has a healthy and wholesome moral tone. He is a force that makes for strength, and sanity, and righteousness.

But it is useless in this brief chapter, even to attempt to mention the names of all prominent Italian authors, nor does a work of this sort require that this should be done, for my purpose is simply to show that the modern Italian character is still informed with the literary and artistic spirit.

The French author, René Bazin, characteristically writes: "The Italian language is so easy for verse! it has so many rhymes in A and O! It is such a singing language! I doubt if there are many young men who have the 'classic license'—*licenza liceale,* who have not turned a sonnet, a serenade, or an elegy. Many of these persevere—which proves their vocation—till past thirty, or even till old age. I have known men mature and settled, who live in the shade of their own lemon trees and write love verses, fiery or tender, which they print themselves, on their own little printing presses, without any desire for fame, giving the book a black cover when the collection is a sad one, and binding in white parchment the inspiration of happier days. Others try to find a place in the reviews, which are always cautious towards lines in rhyme. I would say that northern Italy, and particularly Venetia, is fruitful in poets, were it not that Naples might protest."

It is interesting to note, that just as our own great Civil War gave birth to a new literature, or at least inspired older writers with a new and more patriotic note, writers like Lowell and Whittier and Longfellow and Walt Whitman, so the tribulations of the first half of the nineteenth century through which Italy passed touched the pens of her writers with a fire and tenderness which the more modern writers have scarcely equalled.

Alexander Manzoni and Giacomo Leopardi are two great writers of which this might be said, and it is undoubtedly true, as one has written that "The condemned and exiles of 1821 gave to poetry a new fire of youth, which broke forth in the songs of Giovanni Berchet, Gabriel Rossetti and others. In 1832 Silvio Pellico returned from ten years' confinement in the prisons of Spielberg, and published 'Le Mie Prigione,' a story of his sufferings, so powerful in its patient cadence that it cost Austria more than one lost battle and incited all liberal Europe to pity. His moving tragedy 'Francesca da Rimini,' was full of patriotism." Doubtless the tragic days through which Italy has recently passed will multiply her great poets as well as her historians.

If modern Italy has been surpassed by other nations in the realms of polite literature, she has certainly surpassed as far others in the genius of her musical composers. Rossini, Bellini, Donizetti, and Verdi are four names "any one of which would have brought glory to the nation."

Of Rossini it is said, that he "effected a revolution in music like that of Goldoni in the drama, and one can only appreciate what force, what variety of expression and what fullness and richness of form he added to it by comparing him with his predecessors. His fame can be judged by these lines from the pen of an illustrious French critic: 'After the death of Napoleon there was another man who was the subject of conversation each day from Moscow to Naples, from London to Vienna, from Paris to Calcutta This was Rossini, and his fame knew no boundaries except those of the civilized world."

Bellini, Donizetti, Verdi; every musician and

lover of music knows their names, and realizes something of the debt of gratitude which, because of their genius and industry, America and other nations owe to Italy.

Every traveller from across the water realizes even before the ship comes to anchor in the harbor of Naples, that he has come to a land of song, and the sidewalk serenade, which every evening he will hear from his hotel balcony, confirms the impression. It is true that the voices may often be harsh and unmusical, and that the songs are inspired by the base hope of *soldi,* nevertheless it is the expression of one element in the Italian nature. The returning traveller to America in days of peace had and will have again many an hour enlivened by the songs of the steerage passengers, for almost always there is an amateur musician with a concertina, or at least with an accordion or jewsharp, who is the center of a little group of singers, while the chorus is taken up by the motley throng of men and women, young and old, who surround him. Surely it is a good thing to have something of the music of light-hearted Italy introduced into the more somber body politic of America, even though it come over in the steerage, and may not be of the highest classical type.

It is natural to suppose that the sculptor's art

would flourish in Italy, among a people who have constantly before them many of the great works of antiquity.   We are not disappointed for when we think of Antonio Canova, who belonged to the first half of the nineteenth century, and has been called "the prince of sculptors, and the reformer of art in Italy"; and of Vincenzo Vela, the greatest sculptor of the last half of the century, we realize that the ancient art is not lost.

It must be remembered, also, that the greatest sculptors from other countries have come to Italy to seek inspiration and to perfect their art. America and England are thus indebted to Italy, not only because of the works which her sculptors have produced, but because of the education she has given to their own artistic sons, many of whom have spent their lives in their adopted land.   The world's greatest sculptor of the last century, Thorwaldsen, the Dane, lived for forty years in Italy, and, as I have been writing this chapter, I have frequently looked out of my window at his benign and sturdy figure in marble under the palm trees of the Barberini Palace Gardens.

When Thorwaldsen, after his two-score years in Italy, went back to Copenhagen, he received an ovation in his native city, such as has been accorded to few monarchs or warriors, and around the walls of the Gallery which contains some of his most important work, and where his body lies, in its beautiful flower-decked grave, are painted in fresco, scenes of his humble departure for Italy and of his triumphant return, with the abundant spoil which he had there gathered, a spoil which was the work of his own hands.

In this connection it should be remembered that not only sculptors and painters from other lands have made Italy their home, but men of the widest literary fame have resided here and found their themes. It is only necessary to mention Robert and Elizabeth Barrett Browning, Shelley and Keats, Byron, and our own popular novelist, Marion Crawford.

Though modern Italians have not been so preeminent in painting as in music and sculpture, their artists have been by no means entirely unworthy of the past.

In sciences allied to art Italy has always taken a first rank, especially in astronomy and the application of electricity. Many important discoveries in the starry heavens are due to modern Italians, and we need only mention the name Marconi to recall the most wonderful and startling scientific achievements of the present century. It is difficult to realize that it was only in 1902 that he perfected his invention of wireless telegraphy, so large a place have Marconigrams come to have in the communication of the world. Now from many a headland on the shores of Europe and America and Asia, rise the tall skeletons that receive the messages that fly through boundless space at the command of this great inventor. Every ship of considerable size is equipped with the wireless apparatus, and, in sunshine or storm, through snow or fog, can send their message that "All's well," can warn of storm or icebergs, or send out the distressful call for help to the four quarters of the heavens.

It is interesting to remember also that the most notable triumphs of Marconi have been in linking together America and Europe. His first great success was achieved when, in the last month of 1901, he received a message in Newfoundland, sent from England, two thousand miles away, while a year later he transmitted, from that great wireless station on the bleak bluffs of Cape Cod, a message from President Roosevelt directly to the Queen of England. When we recall the fact that he is only forty-seven years old, his marvellous invention, which has already saved so many hundreds of lives at sea, must be put down to another of the triumphs of young men, for he was not quite thirty when his great discovery was perfected.

CHAPTER VIII

WHY ITALIANS EMIGRATE

The reader who has patiently followed the author thus far in his story of Italy and the Italians may be inclined to ask, Why do these people leave their own favored land? If it is a country so full of interest because of its past, so full of promise for the future, why should men and women who undoubtedly love their native land as we love ours desert it for an untried home far across stormy seas, among aliens in speech and customs?

It would indeed seem to require some very powerful motive to uproot a family from such a country, especially when the difficulties and uncertainties of a new and distant home are remembered. When the individual emigrant is considered, two words may describe the forces which drive him from his native land, and these two words are *poverty* and *taxes*. Perhaps the formula may be reduced to the one word *poverty,* for his poverty is in no small measure the result of the direct and indirect taxes he has to bear.

Necessity is not only the mother of Invention, but of a good many other children, including Emigration. Wages are certainly rising in Italy, as in other parts of the world, but the cost of living is increasing even more rapidly, so that the emigrant is often driven forth by the high cost of living, even though he is in no danger, as are so many in our own land, from the cost of high living.

The latest statistics which I am able to secure show that the wages of engineers in North Italy, where wages were the highest before the war, varied from about sixty-five cents to a dollar and a half a day. Boiler-makers could earn from sixty cents to nearly a dollar and a half. The highest wages paid to firemen were something less than a dollar a day. Skilled master mechanics could earn as much as $1.60, while unskilled laborers had to be content with sixty-nine cents a day.

This was in the north where wages were higher than in any other part of Italy. There is no more death-dealing work, probably, than that in the sulphur mines of Sicily, but even in these mines, if the day laborers earned sixty cents a day they thought themselves well off, while in some of the mines they had to take their pay in produce rather than in cash, which of course al-

lowed another margin of profit to the employer
and a margin of loss for the employee. Marble
quarrying in Italy was one of the great and
unique industries of the Peninsula, but a quarry-
man could rarely expect to earn a dollar a day.
From the present chaotic condition of both wages
and prices no deductions can be drawn. Of
course wages during the war increased in Italy
as in all other lands.

The pay of women in Italy, for the same hours
and the same amount of work, was less than that
of men, though the men's pay was pitiable
enough. Fifty cents a day would have been
considered good pay in a cotton mill for the or-
dinary workman, and twenty-five for the woman
worker, though in some cases she might have
received as much as thirty or thirty-five cents.
This meant for a day of ten hours, as a rule.

The wages of the agricultural laborers, however, are of greater interest to us than those of
any other class, since it is from their ranks,
largely, that the Italian Americans are recruited.

It is refreshing to know that the wages of
such laborers had increased within the twenty
years before 1914 from fifty to one hundred and
fifty per cent. But the reader will ask himself,
What must they have been in the earlier days?
when he learns that the highest pay of an agri-

cultural laborer before the war was less than fifty cents a day, while the women earned less than twenty-five cents, and boys were happy if they found twelve or fifteen soldi (cents) jingling in their pockets at the end of a day's work.   In the region around Naples, the average pay was about thirty-five cents for the men, and half as much for the women, while in Sicily about the same munificent wage was expected.

But what would the total income of a man with a family to support amount to?   It must be remembered that families are by no means small in Italy, four or five children, perhaps, being the average, while the number often runs up to a dozen or more.   The official statistics of agricultural labor, published in Rome a few years ago, gave the highest total average annual income of men at $106.   This was in Piedmont, whereas in the Marches the average income for the whole year was only $52 for the husband and father. The wife and mother and children might among them very likely in many instances have doubled this amount.

These figures alone will explain why more than 300,000 Italians sailed yearly before the war to the United States and other tens of thousands for Argentina and Brazil.

Messrs. Okey and King in their "Italy of To-day," tell us that "the worst offender in the matter of low wages, is the Italian Government itself, which employs women on the railway lines at six cents a day (doubtless only as flagwomen or gate keepers), and plate layers and shunters at an initial wage of thirty-six cents a day, which rises to fifty-nine cents only after twenty-seven years of service." A conservative writer has recently declared that "the starvation wages paid to the lowest grade of government employees in Milan reduces them to a condition only slightly better than that of the unemployed."

It is quite certain that since these statistics, which are the latest I have been able to secure, were gathered, there has been a very considerable rise in wages, a rise which is more than offset by the continuous increase in the price of the necessaries of life.

No wonder that the farm laborer, looking at his hard-earned fifty cents, which was all that ten or twelve hours of back-breaking work with pick or grub hoe had given him, sadly contrasted this meager pittance with the two to four dollars a day which his brother, or his uncle or his cousin was earning on an American railway, or in blasting out an American tunnel.

Of course the real amount of pay a man receives is gauged not only by the amount of money that is given him for his day's work, but also by the amount of the necessaries of life that he can buy with it.   Unfortunately he can buy less in Italy than in most other lands for the same amount of money.   In Rome, for instance, even before the war, flour cost four cents a pound, and sugar fifteen cents a pound.   A friend of mine who lived in Venice for many years told me that with the local duties added, he has frequently had to pay as high as nineteen or twenty cents a pound for sugar.   During the war the Italian sugar bowl was absolutely empty for it took dollars instead of pennies to fill a small one.

As one enters an Italian town, large or small, he is sure to see a little customs house at which the driver pulls up obediently.   The official comes out, peers curiously into the carriage to see if perchance a bag of flour, or a bottle of wine, or a dozen oranges are concealed under the lap robe. If he finds nothing suspicious the traveller is allowed to drive on.   But every load of provisions that enters the village must pay the Octroi duties, or the local tax.   If one drives out from Naples to Pozzuoli, the ancient Puteoli, a few miles distant, where St. Paul landed after his adventurous voyage from Cesarea, he will be inspected as he enters the miserable, decadent town, lest he has brought something contraband from Naples.

When he returns a half hour later, and approaches the invisible Naples frontier, he will be inspected again to see if he has brought something dutiable from Pozzuoli.

When one drives a mile from the ancient walls of Rome to the church of the *Tre Fontane,* or the magnificent basilica of "St. Paul without the Walls," he must, on his return, encounter the excise man.   If he should take the humble trolley car, he would find it held up at the local customs house long enough for the inspector to go through the car, looking suspiciously under every seat, and at every bundle, to see that the majestic Capital of Italy is not defrauded of the duties on a bunch of radishes or a head of lettuce.

Over many a little shop in every Italian city one reads the sign *Sale e Tobacco,* which those uninitiated in the Italian language may perhaps read "Sale of Tobacco."   When, however, they have been a little longer in Italy they will translate it "Salt and Tobacco," and will learn that both of these articles are considered luxuries by the Italian Government which retains a monopoly of them.

Sicily is a great salt producing country, and, if there were no tax upon it, ten pounds could be sold for two cents.   As it is, it costs four cents

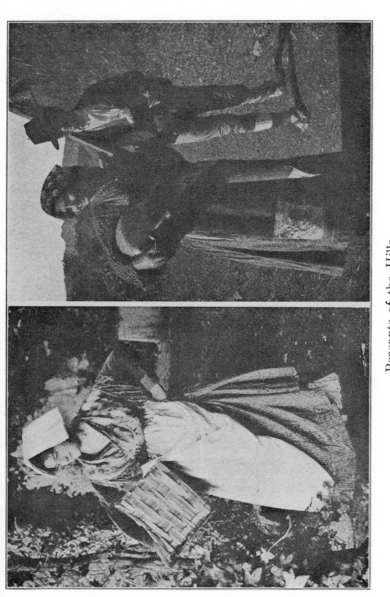

Peasants of the Hills

a pound, and it is said that some of the poorest people in Italy scarcely taste salt from one year's end to the other.   The prevalence of *Pellagra* in some sections is ascribed to the lack of this condiment, and in these regions the tax has been lightened, or altogether lifted.

I recall that once when eating lunch at a small railway junction, where we were obliged to wait some hours for a train, we scattered a little of the salt which the hotel had provided for our hard boiled eggs, upon the table of the waiting room, whereupon the station master, much to our surprise, gathered up every last grain, and did it up in a piece of paper, carefully putting it in his pocket for the seasoning of his own dinner.

It must not be supposed, however, that all necessary articles of food are abnormally high. Meat in pre-war times was no higher than in America, if as high, while vegetables seemed decidedly cheaper.   A bunch of delicious *Finochi* could in the season be bought for two cents; a good cauliflower for twice as much and other vegetables in about the same proportion.   And it must also be remembered that the Italian housewife can make a bunch of *Finochi* and a scrap of meat go a great deal further than can her American sister, for, though the Italians have for the most part one religion, they have a good many kinds of sauces, to vary the gibe of the Frenchman upon English cookery.

In dismissing this question of taxes and high prices I shall venture to quote another paragraph from the authors of "Italy To-day," who have studied the question evidently with great care and thoroughness. Their statistics of course refer to pre-war times for concerning the present abnormal days no figures are reliable.

"The scanty food of the Italian is scantier still, because taxation is out of all proportion to the resources of the country, and protective duties rob the poor to fill the pockets of the rich landlord and manufacturer. According to the calculations of M. Delivet, Italy pays a higher percentage of its income in taxes than any of the larger European States except Spain. The State takes seventeen per cent as against twelve in France, eight in Germany, six in England. Another calculation, founded on M. de Fovilles figures, would place taxation at thirty per cent of income. And in Italy the taxes fall heaviest on the poor. 'It is progressive taxation topsy-turvy,' says Professor Villari, 'the less a man has, the more he pays.' Fifty-four per cent of the taxes, according to the figures of Signor Flora, fall on the poor and working classes. An artisan or laborer, even if he drinks no wine, pays from ten to twenty per cent of his wages in direct or indirect taxation. Wheat pays a duty to the State of $3.37 the quarter. There is a local duty in the larger towns on flour, bread and macaroni, up to ten or fifteen per cent of their value. The adverse exchange and the milling monopoly, which the tariffs ingeniously encourage, raise the price of bread higher still."

As in all highly protected countries, where taxation is abnormally large, every effort is made to evade the taxes, and often with success. The people of the south complain that the manufacturers of the north pay far less than their proportion of the nation's burdens.

How taxes are often evaded, at least in part, is illustrated by a story told me by a friend in Naples, who desired to rent a large room for a religious purpose. The landlord required my friend to sign two leases, one of which was for himself, and obligated her to pay 120 lire, or twenty-four dollars a month rent; the other was for the Government which declared that she paid only sixty lire, or twelve dollars a month. When she demurred, and refused to become a party to this deception, the landlord justified himself by saying that in any event the Government would not accept his statement but would levy taxes on double the amount he declared, so that if the contract shows that he is paid 120 lire a month, the taxes would be a great deal more than was equitable, whereas, if he put down but 60 lire, the tax would then be high, though comparatively fair. Nor was this an exceptional case, for the would-be renter found that to whomsoever she applied she must make out such a double contract.

Such are some of the results of high protection and high tariff in Italy, while another result was formerly seen in the crowded steerage compartments of every Atlantic steamer that was allowed to carry emigrants to America.

CHAPTER IX

In the last chapter some reasons were given, from the standpoint of the individual, for the enormous emigration of Italians to other countries. But this does not tell the whole story, for there are conditions of a nation-wide economic character which compel such an outflow of her citizens, even if the Italians were as great home keepers as their cousins, the French.

We have seen that the area of United Italy is 110,675 square miles excluding her colonial possessions and Italia Irredenta whose boundaries, as I write, are not yet settled. When we remember that into this narrow peninsula are crowded more than thirty-five millions of human beings, that fact alone accounts for the hundreds of thousands of sturdy men and women, who every year from the ports of Genoa, and Naples and Palermo wave their adieu, and often tearful adieu, to their native land.

When a vessel is more than full it must spill over. When the water in a pond reaches the top of the embankment it must find an outlet. The population of Italy has now reached the limit of comfortable subsistence, and gone beyond it. It must spill over into other countries.

In spite of the overflow of her citizens, which in some years has reached three-quarters of a million, and on the whole is steadily increasing, Italy is not being depopulated. She is a virile, vigorous nation. The birth rate is large and shows no indication of material decrease, as in many other lands. If France should lose 700,000 citizens in a year, she would soon be depopulated, for her birth rate barely makes good the death rate, and sometimes falls below it. But at the Italian boundary race suicide ceases, and in spite of sending five millions of her citizens to other lands in the first ten years of this century, she made an actual net gain in population of more than half as many.

In former days those twin demons of slaughter, War and Pestilence, kept down the rapid increase of population, as indeed War has recently done and performed in a less merciful way the same function that the emigrant ship undertook later, in reducing the surplus population of Italy. Under the papal rule it is said that the death rate in Rome was something over sixty in the thousand. Now, if I am not mistaken, it has been reduced more than three-fold, to about sixteen in the thousand, making Rome one of the healthy cities of the world. The draining of the Pontine Marshes, the destruction or circumvention of the mosquito of the Campagna, the improved methods of agriculture, the comparative peace which Italy enjoyed for nearly 50 years until 1916, all these causes upset the equilibrium between births and deaths, and caused Italy's sons and daughters to seek their fortunes in other lands. Of late the War demon is again doing his best to reduce the population of fair Italy and to discourage emigration.

It must be borne in mind that all these emigrants did not desert their fatherland permanently. There is an incoming, as well as an outgoing, tide, especially in the case of the tens of thousands from north Italy who sought work in Germany and Switzerland and France during the harvest months and at certain other periods of the year, most of whom returned when the press of work was over, with as much of their hard earned wages as they had been able to save. There was also an ebb as well as a flood tide in American emigration, as we shall see later, and the steerage accommodations of the Trans-Atlantic liners were at some seasons of the year almost as full on the home-coming ships as on the out-going.   On the whole, however, the coming tide was much smaller than the going.

Consider for a moment longer what the comparative population and area means, in terms of some of our own states.   Cut off the northern third of California, and pack into the rest of that state the thirty-five millions of people who now live between the Alps on the north and the southernmost Mediterranean shore of Italy, and we can imagine what an exodus there would be even from the beautiful shores of sunny California. Even the "Native Sons of the Golden West" would want more elbow room and breathing space.   Crowd these same thirty-five millions of people into the adjoining states of Alabama and Georgia, and they would have more room for their farms and their factories, for their homes and their public institutions, than the people of Italy had before the war.   Or join Iowa and Nebraska in one long state; leave out the western twenty-five thousand square miles of the latter state as being less productive than the eastern portion, and we have a territory considerably larger than Italy from Turin to Syracuse, with a population of only less than one tenth that of Italy.

It must be borne in mind, too, that whereas almost every square mile of Iowa and Nebraska is rich prairie land and capable of cultivation, there are vast mountain sections of Italy, which cannot produce enough herbage for a goat to browse upon. The Apennines run through the center of Italy, from the extreme north to the very end of Sicily, rearing their lofty, and often snow-crowned, peaks above the homes of the peasants in almost every part of the kingdom, reducing, by a very large percentage, the cultivable area. Yet even Iowa, which could probably as easily maintain a population of thirty-five millions as can Italy to-day, begins to feel herself crowded with her two millions of people, and so many of her sons and daughters have gone to other states and to Canada that, during the last decade, her population actually decreased.

These comparisons make the reason for the former outward movement from Italy very plain, and also show why the government did not take measures to restrict this immigration.

At one time the ruling authorities of Italy were decidedly alarmed at the draining away to other lands of so much of its brawn and muscle, and they took strenuous measures to prevent any further increase in the out-going millions. But calmer and wiser consideration convinced the government that, for a country like Italy, there was no other solution of her economic problem, and, if emigration has not been stimulated by the powers that be, it has been wisely guided and regulated.

It soon became evident, too, that while men and women were going out, money was coming back to Italy, not in driblets either, but in millions and millions of lire every year, money sent from the prosperous sons to the old father and mother; money sent back to buy the little homestead, to which the emigrant hopes sometime to return; money for the payment of the mortgage on the home farm, or for the improvement of the homestead.

Moreover, it was found that a very considerable percentage of the emigrants, when they became comparatively well-to-do returned permanently to their fatherland, bringing not only money but new ideas, and improved methods of agriculture, new farming and household machinery, and then, in a multitude of ways, benefiting the fatherland.

It is worth while, in considering this subject, so important to the welfare of our own country, to write, not in glittering generalities, but to give actual figures concerning our new neighbors from Italy. I have before me a publication on the subject, kindly given me by the Italian Commissioner of Emigration, Signor Rossi

In one of the latest years before the war for which complete statistics have been gathered 711,446 Italian emigrants left their native land. Of these the United States attracted considerably more than one third, or 267,637. Next to the United States in popularity with the Italian emigrant, it will surprise many to know, came Switzerland which received more than 89,000 Italians in that year; then Germany and France with something like 75,000 each; but most of these emigrants, as I have before said, returned to their native land when the working season was over.

Of the lands across the sea, Argentina stands next to the United States in popularity with the Italians, though far behind, for only about 70,000, or a quarter part as many as reached the United States, sought the alluvial plains of the River Plate. Brazil attracted half as many as Argentina, or about 35,000, while Canada, in this respect, was a bad fourth and received some 19,000 Italian emigrants.

The year 1912, however, was not by any means a record year for Italian emigration to the United States. The years 1905, 1906, and 1907, all largely surpassed it, for the hard times of 1911 evidently discouraged many who would otherwise have sought a new home within our boundaries. The commissioner had also compiled statistics for

the first half of 1913, and we find the hope of better times largely stimulated the outflow from
Italy, and, in the first semester of 1913, 164,439
emigrants sailed for the United States from
Italian ports.   In the same six months of 1913
about 38,000 returned to Italy, leaving, as will be
seen, a net gain for America of something like
125,000.   The war, beginning in 1914 made further normal statistics of emigration out of the
question.

It will also surprise some of my readers to
know that in some years far more Italians have
returned to their native country from the United
States than sought our shores from Italy.   For
instance, following the panic year of 1907 only
70,000 left Italy for America, and more than
three times as many returned.   In 1911, less than
2,000 more emigrants went out than came back,
while in 1912 more than half as many returned to
Italy, as left her shores, many of them doubtless
finding that in years of depression and dulness the
Stati Uniti was not the Land of Promise that they
had imagined.

The care taken of its emigrants by the Italian
Government is very commendable.   There are
only three ports from which they have been allowed to depart, Genoa, Naples and Palermo, and
then only on ships sanctioned by the government

and complying fully with its stringent regulations. The number which each ship carries is distinctly stipulated, and any violation is severely punished. The amount of space on deck and in the cabin for each emigrant is prescribed. The beds they sleep on, and the blankets that cover them, the food they eat, both as to its amount and quality, are all regulated. An Italian Commissioner and Doctor went out with each load of emigrants, and the doctor was expected to taste of each meal that was provided for the emigrants, to make sure that it was up to the required standard of nutrition. These regulations will doubtless be enforced when emigration is renewed.

Said one emigrant, who had had an experience of more than one voyage across the Atlantic, "When the Commissioner is on board, the steerage is heaven; when he is absent, it is hell." These nervous words may savor of exaggeration, but they tell us forcibly of the difference between the old days of non-regulation and the present.

As the first class passenger looks down from his superior height, on the promenade deck, at the swarming emigrants in the steerage, as he sees the filth with which the deck is often littered, especially after the *al fresco* meals, and, when on stormy days, he sees the wash from the seas sweeping over their quarters, he is inclined to think that the lot of the emigrant, even in these better times, is deplorable enough. Yet on the better ships, he is comfortable in the extreme, as compared with former days, and in good weather, judging from the songs and hilarity which prevail in his quarters he has a much happier time than the first class passengers.

It is well indeed that strict regulations are enforced, for some steamship companies have been merciless enough in their treatment of emigrants. I recall that on one occasion, returning to my home from South America, by way of Europe, I was for some weeks the companion of a great crowd of returning emigrants from Brazil, Argentina, and the western coast of South America. Most of them were Spaniards and Italians. The filth and squalor of their quarters was indescribable. Hearing that there was a dying man in the steerage, I went one day to see if I could do anything for him, and found him in the lowest part of the steerage, and far up in the very bow of the ship. He was dying of consumption, and had been shipped at Valparaiso by some heartless relatives, for the long voyage round the Horn, to his native Italy. He was reduced to a skeleton, and his poor bones were only kept from the bunk on which he lay, by a piece of burlap, while another piece covered him. He could not eat the coarse food of the other emigrants, and had no one to wait on him except the care which his kindly fellow passengers could give him.

I at once sought the captain and told him of the dreadful condition in which I had found this man, and the unspeakably filthy condition of the steerage generally, and intimated that I should report the matter to the authorities on reaching England. He professed great surprise at the condition of things on his own ship, of which, of course, he ought to have been fully aware, and promised to see that the sick man had a steward detailed to wait on him, and that he should have nourishing food as well as care. But, alas, it was too late. Two days more and the poor fellow was dead, and his body consigned to the sea.

His case is doubtless only one of a multitude which other travellers might relate, and it is well indeed, that the Italian government cares for its emigrants after such an excellent paternal fashion both on their outward passage and their return.

CHAPTER X

THE AGREEABLE ITALIAN

What sort of manners will the hundreds of thousands of emigrants from the Peninsula of Italy introduce into their new home across the sea? However Americans may pride themselves on their sturdier and more virile qualities of independence, enterprise and push, we can hardly as yet count ourselves among the most polite nations of the world. In fact, the enterprise and push that have subdued our prairies and spanned our continent with a dozen lines of iron rails, and tunnelled our cities for the subways, have often seemed to push out the gentler qualities of politeness and good breeding.

There is a certain swaggering rudeness, that, by many foreigners, is considered typical of the American; a boastfulness that falls little short of braggadocio, and an insistence on personal rights and privileges, which an undue love of independence has bred. Though these qualities are often exaggerated by the foreign visitor, and though the stories of American manners which Mrs. Trollope and Dickens spread throughout the world, are little less than libels, there must be some foundation for the almost universally prevalent idea that, with all our sterling qualities, we still lack something, as a nation, of the graces and amenities of life.

Will the Italian do anything to improve this racial strain, as, in the generations to come, he mingles his blood with ours, and joins in making the American of the future?

I think it is plain that if we as Americans have something to learn, he has something to teach in this direction.   There is a native politeness about the unspoiled Italian, however poor he may be, that is very charming.   To be sure, he often is spoiled, as we shall see in another chapter, either by his contact with foreigners, or by an exaggerated idea of his own importance, which has come in with the advent of the new Italy, but we can yet find him, in most parts of Italy, with his modest, sunny disposition, his respect for the rights of others, and his desire for their good opinion.   Especially in the country districts do we find this type of Italian, the districts from which, fortunately, come most of those who seek our shores.

As we walk along almost any country road, we are greeted by every peasant with a smile, and a hearty *"Buon Giorno!"* (Good morning) or if he hesitates to presume upon giving us the first greeting a *"Buon Giorno"* from the stranger will light up a more radiant smile and a still heartier return of the greeting.   When I go to dinner in my boarding house, if I meet the pleasant-faced maid in the passage way, she wishes me in a perfectly respectful manner a *"Bon Appetit,"* and when my fellow guests rise from the dinner table, though I may not know one of them, they often bow elaborately, with a pleasant *"Buona Sera"* (Good evening) for their benediction.

All this politeness on the part of the peasants and the servants is usually without any touch of servility.   In some countries one is waited on with the utmost assiduity, but there is the feeling all the time that the servant has his eye on the "tip," and that his politeness is gauged to a hair's breadth by the size of the gratuity that he expects.   A well-dressed man receives twice the attention that his shabby neighbor may expect, and a glittering diamond ring on my lady's finger would greatly accentuate the speed with which dinner is served, and increase the flourish with which the dishes are presented.

In Italy, it is true, the waiters expect their tip as in other countries, but it is accepted as honestly earned wages would be taken, without the suspicion that it is a gratuity for which one should be overwhelmingly grateful. If it is less than the recipients expected, they do not show their displeasure as a more servile waiter in some other countries would do, but accept it with as good grace as possible, hoping for better luck next time.

At an English hotel in Constantinople I have been followed out of the room by an obsequious head waiter, to whom I had already given a fee, demanding a tip for the under waiter, whom I had indeed already paid for his services. Such obsequiousness before the tip, and such insolence afterwards, I can hardly imagine as ocurring in Italy.

In many Italian cities the streets are very narrow, and, at certain times of the day, very crowded, so that it is with difficulty that one forces his way through them, but I have seen very little rude pushing or hustling in these narrow thoroughfares. If one is in a hurry the word *"Permesso"* is usually sufficient to open the way through the densest crowd, and this word seems to be upon the lips of every one. The fishwife with her basket of live eels upon her head, the porter bowed under a heavy trunk upon his shoulders, the errand boy carrying a loaf of bread a yard long under his arm, all intent upon reaching their destination, will have to ask permission to proceed perhaps a dozen times in the course of a short walk, a boon that is always politely asked, and promptly given.

The traveller in Italy naturally gathers some idea of the national traits of character from the hotel servants whom he meets at least three times a day, and they are certainly typical of a large class of Italians, not the poorest, and of course by no means the most cultured. The waiters in their dress suits have often reminded me of the college Glee Clubs at home, when the boys are off on a concert tour, and it would not surprise me to see them line up in a row and give a college yell, or render a college glee. To use a college phrase in this connection, the American University man would have "nothing on" the average Italian waiter in the matter of good looks, self possession, or attractive manners, and I doubt if he could speak half as many languages as the man who brings him his soup and macaroni.

The children of Italy seem to me among the most attractive in the world, and I think this can be said without any qualification. No one can walk through the palm-lined parks of Naples, or watch the small girls skipping rope in the open gravelly space of the *Giardino Reale* in Venice, without being struck by the attractive features, and the pretty manners of the little folks.

Even the poor children in their rags and dirt
have a charm of their own.   Bright black eyes
peep out from under tangled locks.   The swarthy,
oval cheeks are dinted with merry dimples, and
one says a hundred times a day, "If that child
were only well washed and well dressed what a
beauty he would be!"   In their plays, too, they
seem friendly and gentle with one another, and
the care that the big brother bestows upon the
baby sister, though she may be only a couple of
years his junior, is often as touching as it is win-
some.

The older people of Italy have the reputation
of being very fond of children, and of treating
them with great affection and gentleness.   Even
in the poorest rookery, I am told by those who
know, the children are usually loved and petted,
given the best that their parents can afford, and
are treated better than their elders treat themselves.

Patience, it is true, may sometimes cease to be
a virtue, but it is closely connected with good
manners as well as good morals, and the lower
classes in Italy, during the long years when they
have endured a multitude of privations, enormous
taxes wrung from them by unjust rulers, poor
wages and long hours of work, imposed by absentee landlords, have had a chance to cultivate

the virtue of patience in an unusual degree. Frugality, too, as I have said before, has been taught by these hard years of poverty; and contentment, and ability to make the best of one's hard luck, are certainly virtues that are near akin to good nature and good breeding.

That this patient contentment, and this willingness to make the best of things as they are, have not degenerated into apathy and hopelessness is shown by the way in which Mazzini was able to arouse the Italians, from the snow-capped Alps to the sulphur mines of Sicily when he uttered his bugle call for liberty and a united Italy, and when Garibaldi led them during those long twenty years to defeat after defeat, but, at length, to final and glorious victory.

Moreover, every emigrant ship with its prow turned toward the new world, loaded with hopeful, enterprising men, who are willing to face the untried problems of a strange continent, show that with all their patience and resignation to their lot at home, the adventurous spirit of the pioneer has not been crushed out of them.

In closing this chapter I have yielded to the temptation to quote another paragraph or two from the lively and picturesque description by René Bazin, as he tells of his visit to a typical family of the lower orders in a tenement house

in Naples, built by the city to take the place of
another one in one of the unspeakable purlieus,
such as have been a disgrace, and are still, to the
good name of Naples.   In the old slums of Naples undoubtedly this picture would be much less
rosy, but this tells us something of the circumstances and the character of the poorest Neapoli-
tan who has begun to rise in the world, and gives
us some insight into the contented character of
the Italians, which takes what the gods give and
makes the best of it.

One of our party lifts the knocker at a fine,
broad door, belonging to a sort of palace in four
stories.   The *concierge* comes to us through a
paved vestibule very neatly kept.   Opposite is a
square staircase, all in granite.   At the left a
glazed door opens upon a great court, entirely
surrounded by buildings.   We go up as far as
the third story, to have an idea of the medium
apartments in this new quarter.   The building
can   accommodate   thirty-three   families.   The
first apartment that we visit consists of three
rooms, and is occupied by four sisters, of whom
one has two children.   They receive us very willingly on being told that I am a stranger, interested in seeing everything in Naples.   The rooms
were in perfect order; the white walls much decorated with prints or framed photographs.   In the
kitchen a gray turkey was walking about under
the table, and two top-knot pigeons cooed from
the window-ledge.

"How much do you pay, Signora, for this nice apartment?"

"Twenty-six lire ($5.20) a month."

"And you are very well suited with it?"

"Perfectly. Our neighbors have only two rooms, but they pay less—seventeen lire."

The right hand neighbor has no turkey, but he keeps a hen. He is an old journeyman cabinet-maker. He assures us that he has no fault to find with the lodgings, and also that his hen gives him an egg every day. The third household is quite young, and the handsome girl who shows us the apartment does not need to be asked whether she is content. This appears from the smile she gives us, from the coral hair-pin stuck proudly in her crisped hair; also from the absence of turkey, pigeon, or hen. Her man is in the city, and will presently come home. He is a *lustroscarpe*—a bootblack, she tells us.

Upon the whole, the apartments are good, but the price can suit only those who have money saved up, or the very young, who postpone their saving till some later day.

There are still many tenements in Naples unspeakably dark and dirty, but it may be hoped that Bazin's experience at least heralds a better day. When Naples' slums are regenerated it may be taken for granted that the worst of Italy's purlieus have been reclaimed.

A Crowd in Naples

CHAPTER XI

THE DISAGREEABLE ITALIAN

Lest I should seem to the reader to hold a brief for the Italian, and to be able to see nothing but good in his character, I must hasten to add, in order to give an impartial view, that there is a disagreeable type of the national character. These traits, since they lie upon the surface and are seen by any passing traveller, are often apt unduly to prejudice him. He is not likely to see the gentler side of family life, for that, in Italy as everywhere else, is hidden behind the four walls of home; nor is the average tourist likely to know much of the hospitality of the Italians, since ordinarily he spends too short a time in the country to realize its unstinted generosity. One who speaks out of a large experience has said, "The Italians pride themselves upon their hospitality. As a Florentine said to me, 'They know and feel themselves the heirs of a very ancient race, habituated to receive the visits of strangers from every nation, and besides they take great pleasure in making known, admired, and loved, that special corner of the country in which they themselves dwell.' "

But the hasty tripper from America is not in a position to know much of this side of Italian life. He sees the crowds upon the street, the grasping, and often dishonest, landlord of the hotel or restaurant, the beggars that swarm about the church doors, the importunate vendors of post cards and trinkets that he does not want; the "spiders" who stand at the doors of the curio shops, to lure him into their parlors, from which it is difficult to escape without buying some useless article, and he is apt, when he leaves the country, to shake the dust from off his feet, with the devout thanksgiving that there are cleaner and more honest countries in the north, to which he gladly hies himself.

His psalm of thanksgiving for getting beyond its boundaries will be still more emphatic, if he finds that his trunk straps have been stolen, the lock of his trunk picked, and some valuables extracted, with no possible redress from the railway company, which is the Italian government.

Though I believe these are the passing traits of a country which is just emerging from the tyranny of kings and landlords into the freedom of constitutional liberty, yet since they are characteristic of certain types of the Italian of to-day, an impartial writer must not entirely overlook them.

As in most countries which are practical democracies, our own not excepted, there is a class of half-educated Italian youths, who know just enough to look down upon their peasant ancestors, but not enough to be gentlemanly and considerate of others.   The public schools of Italy which abound everywhere, like public schools in other countries, often give a superficial education, which is almost worse than none.   I remember a group of young men, who on one occasion made the long tram-car ride from Castellamare to Sorrento most disagreeable.   We were seated in the non-smoking compartment of the car, when several of them rudely and noisily crowded in and lighted their cigarettes.

One of the ladies of the party suggested to the conductor, who had hitherto taken no notice of the infringement of the law, that *vietato fumare* was posted in large letters in the compartment, whereupon he gently tried to persuade the young men to put out their cigarettes.   The one to whom he spoke did so, whereupon another, in a spirit of bravado, immediately lit his, and took especial pains to puff the smoke into the face of the ladies present, and from that time until the end of the journey, the whole crowd did their best to make things disagreeable. One of them, evidently the "smart Alec" of the party, made various jeering remarks, which perhaps he took it for granted would not be understood, while the others laughed most uproariously at his crude jokes, and all took pains to give to every one the benefit of as much tobacco smoke as they conveniently could, while the conductor was evidently afraid to interfere with their hilarity.

This was undoubtedly an exceptional case, but not an isolated one. These young fellows had been to the public schools, and were able to read and write, while perhaps their fathers and mothers did not know their letters, but they had not obtained the first rudiments of an education in politeness or good manners and in these matters, doubtless, were far surpassed by their unlettered parents. Very likely their children, however, will take the next step, and learn that the good breeding and good manners are the A, B, C of a good education.

It may be a reflection upon the traveller, rather than upon the Italian, but it is nevertheless true that these disagreeable traits are most evident where tourists congregate. In the remoter country districts you will find more courtesy and genuine grace of heart and manner than in the cities and towns crowded with tourists. For instance,

I have never seen such impudent and insolent children as in Amalfi, a little town which, at certain seasons of the year, is overrun with foreigners, for the natural disposition of the Italian child seems usually to be kindly and gracious.

Again, the average Italian peasant has not yet learned the truth of the close juxtaposition of cleanliness and godliness, or if he has, he cares very little for either. As compared with the poorer classes in other countries the poor Italian is often loathsome in his filth and rags. Soap and water seem to be unknown commodities in some sections, and in wandering through the slums of such cities as Naples or Venice, one wonders that the black plague does not sweep off its millions every year, or else he comes to the conclusion that there is very little in the microbe theory, for there seem to be evil germs enough in any one of these streets to inoculate the whole human family.

Closely connected with the filth of Italy, and, indeed, the cause of much of it, is the habit of promiscuous spitting everywhere, and on all occasions. A courtly college president of my acquaintance used to deprecate the habit of certain college students whom he called "young men of great expectorations." His facetious phrase might be applied to nine out of ten of the lower classes of Italian men. The old vendor of papers, opposite my window in the Street of the Four Fountains in Rome, keeps the sidewalk constantly wet in a wide circle around him all the day long, so that the street sprinkler would scarcely seem to be necessary in that region.

"For the sake of health and decency, you are requested not to spit upon the floor," is the pathetic sign in many railway cars, and other public places, yet I have seen a well-dressed passenger actually spit upon the sign, as well as on the floor, apparently unconscious of any wrong, and without the slightest objection on the part of the guard or the other passengers, though some of the ladies drew their skirts about them in mute protest. I have even seen a man sitting on the gunwale of a boat, expectorate into the boat rather than upon the water, as it would seem most natural even for an Italian to do.

Many of the churches prominently post up the sign, "Out of respect for the house of God, you are earnestly prayed not to spit upon the floor," a prayer not always answered by the worshippers.

This disregard of cleanliness is, however, only another passing phase of the evolution of Italy. Such signs as I have alluded to are altogether new, and the average Italian cannot as yet understand their necessity, nor the average policeman the importance of enforcing their prohibition. Some such drastic enforcements of the law as Boston occasionally witnesses, when numbers of people are imprisoned for spitting upon the side- walk, would doubtless go far to remove this nui- sance, and one of these days Italy, in these re- spects, will take her place beside other civilized countries. Already the traveller can see con- stant improvement, even in such cities as Naples and Venice, as he visits them from year to year. Thirty years ago Naples was at times a pest hole, where infectious diseases raged almost un- checked. Now, in spite of the filth of its dark alleys, it is comparatively healthy and wholesome. In Venice, too, I note a great change for the bet- ter in the course of the last three decades, and all this improvement holds out good promise for the future.

The petty impositions practised upon the stranger are even harder for him to bear than the dirt and squalor which he sees in many places. He can step around the filth, and he can shut his eyes to a good deal of it, if he is fastidious, but he cannot avoid the small pilferings which rob him of a soldo here and a lira there.

For instance, he must often make a very hard and fast bargain with his landlord about every possible item of expenditure, or he will find, when his bill is presented, that there are several un-accountable charges, which mine host glibly ex-plains, but which the traveller feels certain are impositions.

He is also pretty sure to have bad money passed upon him. Unless he keeps a very sharp outlook for spurious coins, or for those that are out of date, he will find, when he comes to pay his next bill, that he has on hand a collection of Argentine, Spanish or Greek soldi, or of lire that were coined before 1863, and which will not be taken, or perhaps that his silver coins are of pewter instead of the pure metal.

When one discovers such an imposition and hands back the worthless coins, they are received with the greatest signs of amazement, as though the dealer had never seen such coins before, or possibly he takes it quite as a matter of course, and as a good joke which failed in this particular case, and he smilingly hands the tourist a good coin without apparently the least twinge of con-science.

In a large and apparently very respectable money-changer's office, in the great Galleria of Naples, I once received a bad silver piece in get-ting some gold exchanged. As I sailed from Naples almost immediately afterwards, I did not discover the imposition until too far away to

remedy it at the time. Some two months afterwards, however, I was in Naples again, and,
going to the money-changer, I handed out the bad
coin, saying, "You gave me this when I exchanged my money." Without a murmur of
dissent he immediately handed me good money
for the bad, since the transaction was such an
every day occurrence that he evidently did not
know whether it occurred the day before, or the
year before, but had no question as to the justice
of my demand.

It is interesting to note the extreme caution
which the small dealer exercises when a silver
coin is presented. He will bite it and ring it on
the counter, while sometimes that is not sufficient
and he will take it out on the stone pavement, to
see whether it rings true on stone as well as on
wood. But the traveller himself soon learns
similar caution and eyes suspiciously every piece
of silver that passes through his hands.

There are other little impositions which are
even more annoying. Every one seems to be intent upon rendering some service which you do
not want or need, but which you are expected to
pay for, all the same. The children learn the
trick very early, by plucking a handful of worthless wild flowers, and throwing them into your
carriage as you pass, or by turning cart wheels on

the sidewalk, and then running after you with violent asseverations that you owe them a soldo for their pains.   In many hotels there are several supernumeraries who never seem to do anything for the guest and whom he never sees until they stand hat in hand in the hallway, as he is about to take his departure, but all of whom expect a gratuity.

When you enter a church, one old woman will open the door, while another will pull aside the heavy curtain within, and both will hold out scrawny, dirty hands for payment, though you are quite able to open your own doors, and would much prefer to do so.

In Venice a decrepit old "hooker" is found at every landing-place, who performs the perfectly useless service of holding on to your gondola while you step ashore, though a gondola, of all possible water craft, is the easiest of egress. But this unnecessary service gives him a right to claim a couple of soldi, which you must pay, or else have the uncomfortable feeling that you are cheating a poor old man out of his only means of livelihood.

In one of her short stories of Italian life, Ouida draws a harrowing picture of three starving children from the Roman Campagna, who were found dead on the steps of a church, because they were not allowed to beg for a crust of bread to keep the life within their little bodies. If such a law against beggars was ever enforced in Rome, or any other Italian city, it now seems to have fallen into innocuous desuetude, for you see them in all public places, making the most of their sores and deformities.

It is only fair to remember, however, that these unpleasant features of life in Italy are largely an inheritance of the past. They are the result of centuries of oppression, of poverty and misgovernment. People must live, and, in a crowded country like Italy, the legitimate avenues of earning a living are often very circumscribed, while many of the tricks which seem to foreigners to be impositions, are the immemorial customs of the ages, and seem to the Italian perfectly legitimate ways of earning a living.   ,

The old "hookers" on the Venetian canals, for instance, are superannuated gondoliers, who can no longer scull their black boats through the narrow canals. Many of them receive a small pension, and are allowed to supplement this by "hooking" passengers ashore. Even the beggars have immemorial rights, which it is difficult for the government, with the best intentions, to annul, though it has frequently tried to do so.

Among all these beggars and semi-impostors

I have seldom seen any able-bodied young men or women, and I do not believe that among the emigrants to America will be found many of those who live by their wits or upon the credulity of their neighbors.

In spite of the disagreeable Italian, who sometimes appears to the traveller to be so much in evidence, I still believe that the average emigrant is industrious, thrifty and upright, and that we need him quite as much as he needs us.

CHAPTER XII

It is impossible to describe Italians in one general comprehensive paragraph. There are Italians and Italians, just as there are Americans and Americans. The north of Italy differs from the south as Massachusetts differs from Mississippi or New York from Texas. To describe a citizen of Massachusetts is not to describe a typical American. Indeed, I do not know that there is any typical American, since America produces so many types. Of Italy the same may be said, though her area is so much smaller. But in a general way, and for the sake of convenience, we may learn something at least of the characteristics of Italians by describing the people of the north, of the south, and of Sicily.

The Italian of the north doubtless deserves his reputation for being enterprising, shrewd, and progressive. He is apt to look down upon his southern brother as slow, lazy and ignorant, while the southerner, from the poverty of his meager fields, thinks of his brother in the north as grasp-

ing and rapacious, as obtaining undue govern-
mental favors through the tariff laws for his factories and industrial enterprises, and as escaping
his share of taxation, which falls so heavily upon
the farmer of the south.

Foreigners who have lived long in Italy, and
who are acquainted with both north and south,
have assured me that they like the sunny, good-
natured disposition of the southern Italians better than what they are pleased to call the somewhat top-lofty and sordid character of the north.
The southerner is more dishonest, they will tell
you, in little things, but he has not learned the
art of robbery on a large scale like the "tariff-
fed barons of the north." I give the opinion for
what it is worth. Doubtless all sections have the
defects of their qualities, as well as their virtues,
and the former unhappy political conditions of
the south, the conscienceless tyranny under which
it lived so much longer than the north, accounts
in large measure for the difference in educational
and industrial standards, and for some differ-
ences in moral standards as well.

At any rate, the cities of the north, whatever
their moral and social condition, are, in their outward appearance, much more like the great human hives of America and northern Europe, than
are the cities of the south. Milan and Turin,

The Leading Waldensian Church in Torre Pellice

and some other North-Italian cities might be set down almost anywhere in England or America without much shock to their inhabitants, and with little surprise to the people of these countries, except, perhaps, as they gazed in wonder at the glorious façade of the Milan cathedral, or the gorgeous tombs of the Scaligeri in Verona.

Genoa is a great commercial metropolis rapidly growing in importance, and this commercial growth is constantly making it more like its sister cities, Liverpool, New York or Copenhagen.

Venice must be considered as in a class by itself. It apparently can never grow young or modern, however much commercial prosperity it may enjoy. Its dingy, moth-eaten palaces, its ill-smelling canals, oftentimes filled with garbage that make the smaller ones seem like sewers, its swarms of dwarfed, ragged and dirty degenerates in the poorer sections, cannot have changed much from century to century. Nevertheless, in spite of all these mediæval drawbacks, it is the most fascinating city in Italy. There is no cathedral like *San Marco,* and no square in the world like the *Piazza San Marco,* and in spite of the importunate glass dealers and bead vendors and lace makers, who try one's patience whenever he walks abroad, there is probably no city in Italy to which the tourist's memory returns so often and with such affection, as to the City of the Lagoons.

Rome, Florence, Perugia, Siena and cities of that type in Central Italy, can hardly be classed with either the north or the south.   They all have their peculiar charms, but they are charms that appeal to the student and the traveller, to the archæologist and the lover of art.   They would have the same interest for him if they were found in Russia or South America, for it is not what the people of the present day are doing, but what the people of the past have done, that attracts visitors to their borders.   They are not typical Italian cities, because, though one finds all sorts of Italians in them, they are cities that live largely upon the prowess of their ancestors rather than upon the enterprise and industry of the people of to-day.

Nevertheless, all these cities, and a dozen others that might be mentioned, are instinct with the spirit of New Italy.   They have caught something of the fire of the reformers, and the spirit of the new age.   Almost any one of them would be ashamed to get along without a *Via Garibaldi,* or a *Via Cavour* or a "Street of the Twentieth of September," while from their most important public squares the statue of Victor Emanuel II, with his fierce moustache, is pretty sure to look down upon one from the back of a prancing charger.

Rome, indeed, has become one of the great capitals of the world, and, though it relies none the less upon its antiquities for its attractiveness, it is constantly adding to them new buildings and new streets, which are worthy of its glorious past. I do not think there is a more magnificent memorial in the world than that to Victor Emanuel, when we consider its marble colonnades and gushing fountains which serve as such an effective setting for the glittering golden statue of the first king of United Italy in the Piazza Venezzia at the end of the Corso.

But when all these exceptions are made, it still remains true that the cities and citizens of northern Italy approach more nearly to the type of the cities and citizens of other northern countries, as the years go by.

Manufacturing and commerce are great levellers, either up or down, as the reader may choose to call it; at least they are constantly promoting a similar type of humanity on both sides of the Atlantic. The Italian of these northern cities is alert, pushing, enterprising, like his brother who is engaged in the same pursuits in London or Chicago.

Indeed the northern Italian seems to me far

more like the typical American business man, than like the commercial Englishman. He is not so wedded to his "top hat," or his afternoon tea, for instance, and the throng of merchants in Milan or Turin in their business suits and soft hats, the best of which, by the way, are exported to America in large numbers, could hardly be distinguished from a similar throng in the streets of Boston or Philadelphia.

There is one section of northern Italy, however, which has furnished so much leaven for the rest of the country and the world that it cannot be dismissed without a few paragraphs. I refer to the little section at the very north of the Map of Italy, under the shadow of the Cottian Alps where lie the Waldensian Valleys, the Valley of the Luserna and the Pellice, the Valley of the Angrogna, and the Valley of San Martino. There is no more picturesque and beautiful scenery in the world than is found in these valleys, and the heroic people who live in them, and who at any time during the last fifteen hundred years have been willing to die for their faith, add a supreme touch of interest to this part of Italy.

The Waldensian Church is undoubtedly right in claiming to be the oldest Protestant church in the world, a church that has never been reformed, because it never needed reformation, since, as they claim, it has never wandered from the true faith.

The story of the Waldensians is as romantic, as full of hair-breadth 'scapes and thrilling incidents as any page in the world's history. They claim to have been in existence long before Peter Waldo, who gave them his name, and brought them to the attention of the outside world. The history of the religious life of Europe for eight centuries at least cannot be written without frequent allusions to the Waldensians.

Peter Waldo was awakened to his spiritual condition by the tragedy of a friend, with whom he was talking, dropping dead by his side. He began to study his Bible, and to inquire earnestly of the priest, "Which is the way to God?" The priest finally gave him the same answer that the Master gave to the rich young ruler, "If thou dost wish to be perfect, go sell what thou hast, and give it to the poor." Peter Waldo took the command literally, gave his wife her portion of the estate, and divided the rest of his money among the poor.

Such a course was considered extravagant and erratic, and half crazy, just as Tolstoy's doctrine is considered by some people of to-day. Nevertheless, Waldo's example and teaching had great effect, in spite of his excommunication by the

Bishop of Lyons, and, gradually, a large number of earnest spirits were attracted to his standard, while, after his death, his doctrines and practice obtained a larger and larger following.

The Waldensians were particularly useful in keeping alive the knowledge of the Bible and in circulating its truths, when the Book was forbidden by the ecclesiastical authorities. Waldo himself engaged some priests to translate the Psalms, and the Gospels and other portions of the New Testament into the language of the people, and large sections of these Scriptures, he and his followers learned by heart.

The following interesting report is given by one of the Inquisitors who was sent to exterminate this religion, of the way in which it was propagated among the common people:

They would travel as pedlers, selling silks and pearls, rings and veils. After a purchase has been made, if the pedler be asked, "Have you anything else to sell?" he answers, "I have jewels more precious than these things; I would give them to you if you promise not to betray me to the clergy." On getting the promise, he says, "I have a pearl so brilliant that you can learn by it to love God; I have another so splendid that it kindles the love of God," and so on. Next he quotes such a Scripture passage as this, "Woe unto you that devour widows' houses!" and when asked to whom these denunciations apply, he replies, "To the priests and monks."   Then he contrasts the dominant Church with his own. "Your doctors are ostentatious in manners and dress; they love the highest seats at table, and desire to be called Masters; but our ministers are not such masters.   Your priests are unchaste; but each one of us has his wife, with whom we live chastely.   They fight and kill and burn the poor; we, on the contrary, endure persecution for righteousness' sake."   After some such address the heretic asks, "Examine and consider which is the more perfect religion and the purest faith, whether ours or that of the Romish Church." And thus the hearer being turned from the Catholic faith by such errors, forsakes us.

Upon this incident, alluded to in the Inquisitor's report, Whittier founded his beautiful poem "The Vaudois Teacher."   This sturdy body of Christians endures to the present day, and is indeed growing stronger and more influential, being the chief Protestant factor in the religious life of Italy.

A few years ago they dedicated a new and magnificent church in Rome, the gift of a wealthy and benevolent American lady, Mrs. John Stewart Kennedy, and their influence is felt not only in their beloved Waldensian Valleys, but throughout the whole length and breadth of Italy, and even in the remote districts of Sicily.   They still maintain many of their early characteristics, and are justly proud of the memory of their martyred ancestors.   Milton's   famous   sonnet   on   the slaughter of the Waldensians, in 1655, is a classic that tells something of the sufferings and the heroism of this ancient people.

Avenge! O Lord, Thy slaughtered saints, whose bones
Lie scattered on the Alpine mountains cold!
Ev'n them who kept Thy truth, so pure of old,
    When all our fathers worshipped stocks and stones,
    Forget not!   In Thy book record their groans;
Who were Thy sheep, and in their ancient fold
Slain by the bloody Piedmontese, that rolled
    Mother with infant down the rocks.   Their moans—
The vales redoubled to the hills, and they
    To heaven.   Their martyred blood and ashes sow
O'er all the Italian fields, where still doth sway
    The triple tyrant; that from these may grow
A hundred fold, who, having learned Thy way,
    Early may fly the Babylonian woe!

CHAPTER XIII

The Italian of the south is of more practical interest to the American than his brother of the north, since the great majority of our Italian immigrants hail from the provinces to the south of Rome. Thus while in a recent year something over 10,000 emigrants went to the United States from Piedmont, some 2500 from Liguria, and less than 6000 from Lombardy, the Campania, which includes the region about Naples, sent us over 51,000, or about three times as many as the three great northern provinces put together. At the same time the Abruzzi, which is a province to the north of Campania, sent us over 31,000 emigrants, and Calabria, the most southerly province of Italy proper, dismissed over 25,000 of her citizens to our shores.

Of course the economic reasons for this tremendous emigration from the south are easily understood. The southern provinces are poorer than the northern, far more crowded with those who are living from hand to mouth, and with far smaller opportunities for the common people to rise in the world. To such people America is naturally the land of their dreams. It is the Continent of Opportunity, and the uncle, or brother, or cousin who has succeeded in the new world, does not find it difficult to beckon the brother or uncle or cousin, who was left behind, across the sea.

It must also be borne in mind that the Italian of the north has other outlets for his energies in foreign countries nearer at home, for during the same year nearly 60,000 Lombardians went to Central Europe, to countries like Switzerland, Germany, Austria and France, while almost 100,-000 Venetians (people of the province of Venetia) found temporary homes in the same countries. But these men and women largely return to their Italian homes, after the harvest seasons in central Europe, and can hardly be considered emigrants in the same sense as those who go to America, who, for the most part, burn their bridges behind them, or, to change the figure, take their lares and penates with them.

To Americans, therefore, southern Italy and Sicily must be considered of supreme interest, since it is from these sections that are coming and will come the influences, which, for better or worse, will affect our national character

The people of southern Italy have long illustrated the old proverb, "Give a dog a bad name, and hang him," and too few inquire whether the poor dog really deserves the bad name, and the capital punishment that results from it.

For instance, an influential author writing about the condition of the southern provinces a few years ago, conditions which, as compared with the industrial conditions in the north have not greatly changed, declares that, "It is easy to illustrate the contrast between the industrial progressive, democratic north, and the agricultural, stagnant, feudal south where (leaving aside the buffer central states) illiterates are nearly thrice as many, where there are three or four times as many murders and violent assaults, where gambling in the State Lottery is twice as rampant, where the death rate is higher, where books and newspapers are comparatively rare, and postal correspondence is less than half. Here the poverty of Italy becomes destitution. The wealth per head is only half as great. The returns of land-tax, income-tax, stamp-duties, consumption of tobacco, witness to its relative inferiority. The land is comparatively a monopoly of the few. Individualism runs riot; there is little mutual trust, or co-operation, and industry goes limping in consequence. It is a land for the most part given over to inertia, with little ambition of better things."

But there is another side to this dark tapestry. It is these very conditions that drive the southern Italian to our shores, and to say that a land is stagnant and unenterprising and given to violence and gambling is not to say that all the inhabitants can be thus described. To some sections of our own country these adjectives might be applied. It is the very people who are not stagnant or unenterprising who buy tickets for America. The fact that they do this is proof positive of a certain degree of enterprise, and though the murderer or other criminal may occasionally slip through the meshes of the law and embark for America, with the present stringent regulations, and their strict enforcement he is not often likely to do so.

The record of every emigrant is well known to the inspectors, and steamship companies will not often take the risk of providing double passage for a criminal, or one diseased, when they remember the hawk-eyed inspector who will greet them at Ellis Island. A country that would not admit a Maxim Gorky, who is considered by some the greatest living author, because of his matrimonial irregularities, and which bars out a celebrated actress for the same reason, is not likely to be very lenient to less distinguished immigrants.

It cannot be denied that the immigrant from southern Italy is usually poor, and often in the past has been illiterate, but these are by no means heinous sins, when we consider his lack of opportunities, nor are these the kind of men whom a country that needs their brawn and muscle, and that can remedy their defects in education, should bar from its shores.   Industry, thrift, temperance, enterprise,—these are qualities which may well make up for any amount of poverty or illiteracy, and these are the qualities which the immigrant from southern Italy largely brings with him when he seeks a new home.   The new literacy law will doubtless keep out many a worthy, hard-working Italian whose only fault is a lack of opportunity to learn.

That his poverty is indeed often extreme is shown by some statistics carefully gathered concerning the expenses of a day laborer's family of five persons in a region to the south of Rome. Such a family it was found, on the average, would eat each week about twenty-one pounds of wheat flour, seventeen pounds of Indian meal, nineteen cents worth of oil and condiments, four cents worth of meat and bacon, four eggs, half a pound of salt, while the total cost of living expenses of this family of five per week would be $2.13, or about forty-two cents for each person. This would include the weekly proportion of the $9.00 a year spent for clothes and shoes, and the $2.60 a year spent for firewood. These figures, which are the actual budgets of actual families, are of themselves eloquently convincing as to the reasons why the steerage accommodations of the emigrant ships that turn their prows to America were, before the war, crowded to the utmost. Doubtless the world-wide rise in the cost of living vitiates these figures, but as compared with other countries the proportions remain true.

Let me describe what a traveller actually sees as he journeys through the provinces of southern Italy, not on a rapid express train, with an entrancing novel in his hand at least to divide his attention with the entrancing scenery, but as he goes to some out of the way place which the foot of the tourist rarely treads, and where he sees his future fellow countrymen as they actually are in their own homes. I have made some such journeys on purpose to get a first-hand impression of the Italian of the south.

Let us go first to the inland city of Benevento. It is a place of some 20,000 inhabitants, lying southeast of Naples, and is famous in ancient story, as are so many of the little-known towns of

the Italy of to-day.   Through this town passed
the great Appian Way, over part of which St.
Paul made his toilsome journey when, as a prisoner, chained to a Roman soldier, he travelled
from Puteoli to Rome.   Here in Benevento
we find a splendid Triumphal Arch erected to
Trajan, as fine as any in Rome, and even in a better state of preservation than the Arch of Con-
stantine or that of Titus.   Trajan himself never
saw it, or the marble delineations of his triumph,
with which it is covered, for he died before returning from the victory which the arch cele-
brates.

We started from the seashore city of Salerno,
and for many miles as the road led northward
through the hills we were impressed with the incredible patience, perseverance and industry,
which in many places alone made agriculture at
all possible.   The barren hillsides were often terraced almost to the very top with twenty, thirty
or forty long parallel lines of terraces, built up
with stones to hold the soil from slipping back
into the valley.

But the soil, though meager in quantity, was
evidently rich in quality, for vegetables of all
kinds, vines and olive trees flourish on these
mountain sides.   Many of these hills of southern Italy remind me more of the terraced Andes

in Peru than any others that I have seen, terraces built by the industrious Incas before the disastrous and cruel Spanish invasion. The difference is that the terraces of the Incas are but the ruins of the industry of a past civilization. Since the Spanish invasion they have become dry and verdureless, but the terraces of southern Italy are fresh and green in their spring foliage, and abundant in the golden fruitage of autumn.

Evidently the people have made the best of such resources as they have. Now and then the train makes its way through a long and fertile valley, every square foot of which is cultivated. Great teams of white oxen with their long, branching horns, are ploughing the mellow soil, or twenty peasants in a row, both men and women, with their gleaming, sharp-pointed spades, are turning the soil for the spring planting.

The words of the Psalmist never seem more appropriate than when one looks upon these rich valleys, and these girdled hills made so productive by the infinite toil of the peasant. David, if he wrote the sixty-fifth Psalm, it would seem might have been looking at these same charming south Italian landscapes when he wrote, "Thou crownest the year with thy goodness; and thy paths drop fatness. They drop upon the pastures of the wilderness, and the hills are girded with joy. The pastures are clothed with flocks; the valleys also are covered over with grain; they shout for joy, they also sing."

When we reach Benevento, it must be admitted that some of the poetry disappears from the scene, especially while we are shown into a dirty and stuffy room in the "best" hotel in the city. Benevento has one broad street, which, of course, is called the *Corso Garibaldi*. The side streets are narrow, mean and dirty alleys. Besides the great Triumphal Arch of Trajan the city possesses some objects of interest to the student and traveller, like the old castle, now the municipal building, the ancient cathedral with its bronze doors, etc., but it is modern Benevento that most interests us.

We see a curious mixture of things modern and ancient. We are reminded of America and Italy both, at every turn. From one shop we see great rings of bread, or long loaves tied to a pole, a dozen or more on one stick, while bladders full of lard, and curious looking piles of cheese remind us that we are still in the heart of Italy. The next store may look quite like an American shop, as seen in a town of the same size, with the same variety of miscellaneous goods, and the American influence is even seen in the prices of the hats in the shop window, marked *"one dolari, five and one half lire,"* the sign evidently meant to attract the attention of the returned emigrant, who could reckon in dollars and cents as well as in lire and soldi.

I saw no saloons in the American sense of the word, an immense improvement in that respect over the average town of twenty thousand in America before prohibition abolished the saloon, and though the streets were crowded with people, and there was much hilarity and merriment far into the evening, I saw no drunkenness. This town, let us remember, is in Foggia, which is considered one of the backward sections of Italy.

The next day we travelled on to Telese, a dirty and forlorn little village, and alighted from the train at a station which was in every way worthy of the village which it served, for it was as dirty and forsaken as could well be imagined. The cold spring rain came down spitefully in showers, and the wind whistled through the broken panes of glass, for there was scarcely a whole one in the station. The third class waiting room was for some reason inaccessible, and the first class was occupied by peasants who dozed and smoked and spat in turn, though some of them seemed to sleep and spit at the same time.

A few miles beyond Telese lies Castelvenere,

The Leaning Towers of Bologna

the little hamlet for which we were bound, and here were most evident some of the causes which drive the people to America. The soil in many parts seemed very poor, and some of it was actually uncultivable. Some of the fields and hillsides looked as rocky and scrubby as the poorest hardscrabble acres in New Hampshire, but even in these a few goats were browsing, and wherever there was a chance to "stick in a tree," or plant a seed, the most was made of it. Some of the hillsides, wherever soil was procurable, were terraced, and the people who live here, even to wring the hardest kind of subsistence from the soil, must be industrious and patient to the last degree.

Much has been written of "Brave Little Holland," whose inhabitants have wrested her soil from the sea. With equal truth, the same adjectives might be applied to this part of Italy where the people, when we consider the increased burden of taxation which they bear, must have a much harder time than in Holland to make both ends meet.

The hamlet of Castelvenere consists of one street, lined with tall stone houses, dirty, cold and cheerless, which seemed especially gloomy, in the driving rain which greeted us on our approach. How any cheerful being could come out of such tomblike structures, it was hard to imagine, and yet the children looked happy and hearty, and mud pies were evidently as dear to their hearts as in more genial localities.

As we drove back to the station at Telese we found only one man in the vicinity who could speak any English, and that very much fractured. He told us that he had been two months in America and was going back again as soon as he could. His reasons for preferring America, were, I regret to say, more mercenary than patriotic. "Italy no good," was his remark. "In America, two dollars there every day; in Italia two or three lire" (forty or sixty cents). The emigration agent in this vicinity apparently does a land-office business. His name is Giuseppi Venditti. He is evidently the chief man of the neighborhood, a good Waldensian who has built a chapel for his faith, near his own house. On every blank wall we saw his name on huge posters, and though we were not fortunate enough to find the gentleman himself at home, his hospitable wife urged us to enter their home, the best in all Castelvenere, and share their *colazione*. We were not able to accept her invitation, but, as we looked around upon the poverty-stricken country, we felt sure that her husband was showing his practical religious faith, not only in building a chapel, but in making the way easy for some of his countrymen to reach more fertile, if not fairer, fields, in the lands across the seas.

CHAPTER XIV

THE WORLD'S WINTER PLAYGROUND

More and more every year, is the beautiful island of Sicily becoming the winter playground of the world. Since brigandage has been so largely suppressed, and the traveller is safe in any part of the island, it is becoming each year more popular with tourists who are looking for a balmy and genial climate, charming scenery, and glimpses of men and things, customs and costumes with which they are unfamiliar at home.

Sicily has indeed many attractions for men of different tastes. The archæologist will rejoice in the antiquities of Syracuse and Girgenti. The lover of history will gladly tread in the footsteps of the leaders of many races, who have given to Sicily three thousand years of recorded and often thrilling history. Says Freeman, the historian, "The greatest powers and nations of the world have in several ages fought in Sicily and for Sicily. Their Sicilian warfare determined their history elsewhere. In this way, the history of Sicily is one of the longest and most unbroken histories in Europe."

The mathematician and the inventor will make his way to Syracuse and gaze with especial interest on the striking statue of Archimedes, with his burning glass and his screw, and will remember that here lived and fought and died, in the defence of his native city, the great pioneer of inventors, who declared that if he had but a place to stand, a lever long enough and a fulcrum strong enough, he could move the world. The mere lover of beautiful scenery, who is off for a happy holiday and who cares little for archæology, or history, or mathematics, or art, will go to Taormina, and will gaze in rapture on the magnificent view of sea and shore there spread out before him.

The art lover, too, will find much to attract him in some of the cities, especially in the magnificent mosaics of Palermo, and the man who knows his Bible will be glad to remember that St. Paul, himself, spent three days in Syracuse, after his tempestuous voyage across the Mediterranean and his shipwreck on Malta, when on his way with his soldier guard to imprisonment and martyrdom in Rome. Thus Sicily, unlike many holiday resorts, holds peculiar joys for all sorts and conditions of people, and we do not wonder at its growing popularity, or that its attractions bring tourists from the ends of the earth to its shore.

The island is a little larger than the state of
Massachusetts, but in other respects is about as
far removed from the old Puritan Common-
wealth as can well be imagined, in spite of the
fact that thousands of Sicilians have often in a
single year sought the hospitable shores of Massachusetts Bay.   Instead of a recorded history of
less than three hundred years, like the Land of
the Pilgrims, Sicily, as I have said, has a recorded
history of over three thousand years.   Instead
of an early ancestry almost entirely English, like
Massachusetts, she has a mixed ancestry, drawn
from more than a dozen different and powerful
nationalities of the ancient world.   Instead of
the characteristically sturdy apple tree of the
Bay State, Sicily produces the more delicate and
tender orange, lemon, fig, loquot and olive, and
she replaces the pine tree with the palm.

But more particularly in her institutions, and
in the every day life of her people, is Sicily at
the furthest remove from a typical American
state.   Until recently she has been terribly mis-
governed, and deprived of almost every sem-
blance of self-rule, and a few years of comparatively good government cannot hope to overcome
the tyrannies and corruptions of centuries.

From this island, small in area, but occupying
so large a place in the world's history, have come,

and will come again, tens of thousands of her sturdiest and most enterprising peasantry every year to our shores. Its history, therefore, and its people and their characteristics may well be of peculiar interest to the American.

Even before we step on Sicilian soil, as we approach the Straits of Messina, we are reminded that we are coming to a classic land, a land of myth and story and poetry, for at the very gateway of the Straits, which separate Sicily from the mainland of Italy, we are met by Scylla and Charybdis, the dreadful rock and whirlpool of ancient times, which steam power and a better knowledge of navigation have shorn of all their terrors, and at the same time of all their romance. It may be interesting to the reader to recall Homer's account of the Rock and the Whirlpool, before we further introduce him to the Island which they so long guarded. Writing of Scylla, Homer said,

The rock is smooth and sheer, as it were polished, and in the midst of the cliff is a dim cave turned to Erebus, toward the place of darkness, whereby ye shall steer your hollow ship, noble Odysseus. Not with an arrow from a bow might a man in his strength reach from his hollow ship into that deep cavern; and therein dwelleth Scylla yelping horribly. Her voice indeed is no greater than the voice of a new-born whelp, but a dreadful monster is she, nor would any look on her gladly, not if it were a god that met her. Verily she hath twelve feet dangling down, and six necks exceeding long; and on each a hideous head, and therein three rows of teeth set thick and close, full of black death. Up to her middle she is sunk, far down in the hollow cave, but forth she holds her head from the dreadful gulf, and there she fishes, swooping round the rock, for dolphins or sea-dogs, or whatso greater beast she may anywhere take.

And here is Homer's description of Charybdis, which lies on the Sicilian side of the Strait, while Scylla keeps guard on the Calabrian side. Of this rock, at whose base lay the dreaded whirlpool, Homer wrote:

Thou couldst send an arrow across. And thereon is a great fig tree growing, in fullest leaf, and beneath it mighty Charybdis sucks down black water, for thrice a day she spurts it forth, and thrice a day she sucks it down in terrible wise.

Tame and peaceful enough are these ancient terrors to-day. But a more real enemy of mankind looms in view as we gaze southward from Messina, to the mighty, snow-capped volcano of Ætna. The Sicilians may well live in dread of

Genoa Near the Great Quays

this monster, which needs no poetic and mythical horrors to enhance its destructiveness.

No less than eighty great eruptions have been recorded during the last two thousand years, some of them of frightful violence.   As far back as the year 396 B. C. we read of its belching forth flames and lava, and of the destruction which overwhelmed thousands of Sicilians.   In 1169 A. D. the people of Catania, which lies at the very foot of Ætna, and which has always suffered most from its eruptions, were celebrating the Feast of St. Agatha in the great cathedral.   The enormous church was filled with people, some thousands in all, every one of whom, it is said, including the bishop and forty-four Benedictine monks, perished, while in the city of Catania, some 15,000 in all were overwhelmed by the fiery flood.   Mr. Will S. Monroe, in his interesting and valuable volume, "Sicily, the Garden of the Mediterranean," gives this graphic account of the eruption of 1669, based upon the story of Alfonso Borelli, who was at the time one of the professors in the University at Catania.   This account may well stand as typical of many another awful scene of destruction for which Ætna has been responsible.

On the morning of the eighth of March the sun was suddenly obscured and serious earthquakes, which continued for three days, were felt. A fissure twelve miles long, six feet wide, and very deep, opened on the side of the mountain and from this issued a bright light.

Six mouths opened on the line of the fissure, which emitted vast volumes of smoke accompanied by noises which could be heard forty miles away. Soon a new crater, a mile below the others, opened, and from this red-hot stones, sand, and ashes were thrown into the air and covered the country for a distance of sixty miles. A torrent of lava with a front of two miles issued from the new crater. It flowed toward Catania and destroyed fourteen towns, and many thousands of people in its progress.

Just before reaching Catania the lava stream undermined a hill covered with wheat fields which it carried forward a considerable distance. The walls of Catania were sixty feet high, but it soon rose to the top and fell into the city in a fiery cascade. When it finally reached the sea, it caused the waters to boil violently and great clouds of steam arose carrying up quantities of scoriae. It filled up the port, and destroyed most of the city.

In the city of Messina, which is the first Sicilian town that the tourist sights when passing through the Straits, he sees melancholy evidence of the awful powers of nature in her destructive moods, for here is the city which, on December

28, 1908, suffered the greatest disaster of modern times.   It is indeed still a sad sight, with its
deserted streets, its piles of crumbling ruins, its
hollow, silent houses, imposing often in their outward appearance, with carved stone cornices and
balustrades, but hollow and empty within, since,
in that awful disaster, the floors and roofs often
fell in while the outer walls remained intact.
Comparatively little has yet been done to rebuild
the city.   The *American Campo,* as it is called, is
a quarter covered with small wooden houses sent
from America ready made, when the hearts of
our people were touched by the awful woes of
Messina.   These houses are little more than
huts, such as would shelter our cows or hens at
home, but they were a wonderful boon to the
people of Messina at the time, and they seem
loath to leave them for more substantial dwellings.

But Sicily is not altogether a land of volcanoes
and earthquakes.   It has charming little valleys,
and great stretches of fertile soil, where the vine
and the olive flourish, and where citrus fruits of
all kinds attain their full perfection.   Here, too,
are numberless ravishing glimpses of the sea and
shore.   Here we find a climate which might make
even southern California envious, and here are
temples and palaces of the olden days, which

show by their ruins what mighty people have inhabited Sicily.

To indicate how desirable Sicily has been considered by the nations of antiquity, it is only necessary to state that no less than fifteen different nations have fought for the possession of the land, and have occupied her soil for a longer or shorter period during these last three thousand years. While this enumeration, as Mr. Monroe remarks, does not include the earliest inhabitants, the Sikans and Sikels, and the Elymians. These fifteen great nations in the order of their occupation, before Italy, fifty years ago, established its dominion over Sicily, are the following: Venetians, Greeks, Carthaginians, Romans, Byzantines, Goths, Vandals, Saracens, Normans, Germans, Anjouans, Arragonese, Spanish Bourbons, French, and English, and each it has been truly said "has left its trace on the Island." What country has had a more varied history! What nation has had so many masters! In what people are there so many strains of heroic blood mixed? What these people are to-day, how they live, their faults and their virtues, and what we may expect them to contribute to America, I shall try to tell in another chapter.

CHAPTER XV

For more than five years emigration from Italy has been almost entirely suspended, but in the year 1912 almost 100,000 people from the comparatively small island of Sicily distributed themselves over the face of the earth, seeking new homes in Europe, Asia, Africa and America. No less than thirty-seven different countries received a contribution of her stalwart laborers in that one year. More than 15,000 sought Argentina; something over three thousand looked for a home in Brazil; Tripoli, the new province of Italy, lured about one thousand to her shores; Canada received about the same number, while more than two-thirds of all, to be exact, 64,243, sought the *Stati Uniti,* as they designate our country. In 1913 still more Sicilian emigrants landed in America.

These figures are more impressive when stated in other terms or when we remember that Sicily, in a single twelve months, sent out from her shores as many people as would make up the full quota of the population of Charleston, S. C., or the thriving manufacturing towns of Brockton, Mass., or Fort Wayne, Ind., or the capitals of Nebraska or Pennsylvania.

This only in a single year, while a constantly larger stream in the future will doubtless flow to us from this one island of the Mediterranean. It is well worth while for us, then, to consider who these people are, who every year have been coming to us in numbers large enough to constitute a thriving city of the second class.

When a Sicilian is mentioned, doubtless many an American conjures up a picture of a ragged, dirty, low-browed assassin, with his ever ready stiletto and pistol, and he mutters the frightful words *"Mafia"* and *"Camorra"* without having any well-defined idea what they mean. Of all the immigrants to our shores, doubtless the Sicilian has the worst reputation, but let us ask ourselves if he deserves it.

It is easy enough to make out a very bad case for the Sicilian. In no part of Italy is there so much poverty, and ignorance, and so many crimes of violence. Alexander Dumas once described the poverty of Sicily in his own unapproachably graphic manner:

Here poverty is seen in all its hideousness, with fleshless, feeble limbs and cavernous, feverish eyes. It is hunger with its cries of suffering, with its eternal death-rattle—hunger that triples the years on the faces of young girls; hunger that makes the young Sicilian maiden, at an age when in all other lands women are beautiful with youth, seem falling into decrepitude; hunger more cruel, more implacable, more deadly than debauchery that blasts and withers, without affording, like debauchery, the gross and sensual comforts of its rival in destruction.

This is probably the worst that can be said of Sicilian life by a master of words, and it was doubtless written at the time of the Bourbon domination, when Sicily had sunk to its lowest estate. I can testify from personal observation in many parts of Sicily that the condition of affairs is by no means so bad under the enlightened and progressive Italian rule, though, of course, there is still much left to be desired, and it can hardly be expected that a nation will be born in a day. To cleanse, to purify, to educate, to enlighten a people who have been so long ground down in the dust by the heel of the oppressor is a matter of decades and centuries, rather than of years. There is, of course, plenty of poverty and distress still in the island, but it is not the hopeless destitution of earlier years.

The Sicilians are not without their ideals and their ambitions. They, too, were thrilled by

Garibaldi's bugle notes, for here he led his most successful revolt. They, too, were inspired by Mazzini's eloquent appeals for brotherhood and liberty, and there are no more ardent supporters of the new régime than the Sicilians.

America, also, has opened a new door of hope to Sicily, as we have already seen, and every able-bodied peasant who has no black record of crime hanging over him, knows that, if he cannot make a living at home, there is a broader land beyond the Mediterranean and the Atlantic, where he can make or mend his fortune.

A sufficiently dark, but more accurate description of the Sicilian home of to-day is the following, by a recent writer:

The dwellings of the Sicilian peasants are little more than hovels. They usually have only one room, often windowless, or lighted only by the door, for windows are a luxury in Sicily; good glass is very expensive and cheap glass cracks in the hot sun. The floor is of worn stone, the walls are rudely plastered and the only heat in winter comes from the small charcoal brazier that is used in preparing the food. An iron bedstead, a shaky table, and a few rude chairs cover the furnishings. The walls are decorated with political caricatures taken from the newspapers, advertisements of steamship lines to the United States and South America, and a wooden crucifix suspended in the corner. Over the doorway one often sees a rude carving of the Mother of Christ and her Child, or a great cross scrawled in the whitewash. But the Sicilian peasants have learned the art of living out of doors. The street is their drawing room.[1]

Let me place side by side with this a more pleasing picture of Sicilian family life as Norma Lorimer, who has written "By the Waters of Sicily," describes the purchase of the wedding jewelry by a Sicilian family:

I have more than once seen a little family conclave, lasting the greater part of the day, taking place in some quiet jeweller's shop. A table is placed in the middle of the floor, and the family —which usually consists of three generations at least—take their places at it with an air of dignified importance. The mother of the bride is draped in the usual fine, black cashmere shawl, but the glossy head of her pretty daughter is of course hatless; her parents can afford to buy her some fine gold trinkets for her dowry, but she has not risen to the social position of wearing a hat. A bright scarf of many colors will be worn over her hair on the journey home.

The jeweller does not expect the party to hurry over their purchase; what has taken so long to save must not be spent too quickly. The whole shop is turned out for them to examine, although

[1] From "Sicily, the Garden of the Mediterranean."

the article of their choice has been decided upon at home for some months past. Dear, simple people, no one is left out upon this important occasion. The old family servant is there, and so are one or two good neighbors. I can imagine the bare little Sicilian home made bright that night by the presence of the wonderful necklace.

If the Sicilians are poor, and many of them even destitute, we must remember that it is not chiefly their own thriftlessness that has made them so, certainly not intemperance, which brings so many Anglo-Saxons to the gutter, for all agree that intemperance is not a crying Sicilian vice, but it is the hard conditions under which they have lived, their crowded soil, their high taxes, their inability to provide modern agricultural implements,—for here, as in so many other directions, the "destruction of the poor is their poverty," as Solomon declares. Moreover, America must take her share of blame for the poverty of Sicily, though we have unconsciously contributed to it, for one by one, we have robbed her of a portion of her market for her chief exports, by producing and exporting the same things ourselves.

At the time of our Civil War a considerable quantity of an excellent quality of cotton was raised in Sicily, but when the war was over and our broad cotton fields began to expand still further, and our improved processes of harvesting and ginning the cotton constantly reduced its price, Sicily could no longer compete, and this source of revenue was lost. Formerly, America was the best market for Sicilian lemons and oranges, but California and Florida came to the front with their delicious citrus fruits, and Sicilian lemons and oranges have had to take a second place in our markets. Still, the lemon trees of Catania and Palermo are so prolific, each producing on an average from one thousand to twelve hundred lemons in a year, that this course of revenue, though diminished, is by no means lost, since Continental Europe remains a good customer, and, moreover, a third of the lemon crop, since the loss of much of the American market, is made into citrate of lime.

Formerly, sulphur, which is the chief mineral found in the island of marketable value, was a great source of revenue to Sicily. Thirty thousand men were employed in this industry, and a dreadfully unwholesome, blighting industry it is too. They manage to produce some 400,000 tons of sulphur every year. Of late years enormous deposits of sulphur have been discovered in Louisiana, and we no longer need to send to Sicily for that evil smelling product of the earth.

This may, in the end, be a good thing for Sicily, if it turns the attention of her people to more wholesome and healthful occupations than sulphur mining, for we are told that "the sulphur miners represent the lowest type of the Sicilian population. They are often recruited from the criminal classes, and they enormously increase the illiteracy, crime, and vice statistics of the Island."

But I shall be asked, What of the *Mafia* and the *Camorra,* of which we hear such dreadful tales? One would think, from the way in which some people shudder when these words are spoken, that they supposed that every Sicilian belonged to one of these organizations, and went about with a stiletto in his sleeve, ready to plunge it into the heart of any unoffending neighbor. But, as a matter of fact, the *Camorra* has nothing to do with Sicily. It is an evil institution of Naples alone. It has been rightly called "a vicious and malodorous conspiracy of the dissolute and criminal poor, who live by blackmailing their fellow poor, and selling their electoral services to the government or the local deputies. It has its tariff of blackmail on boatmen, porters, prostitutes and gamblers. It drives a lucrative trade in unspeakable horrors, and such is the traditional fascination which it has on the imagination of the citizens that its sway is often absolute, and the police are glad to call in its authority where they are powerless."

If the *Camorra* is a product of Naples, the *Mafia* seems indigenous to Sicily. Someone has called the *Mafia* "a degenerate form of chivalry," and it is not unlike the Ku Klux Clan, or the organizations among the mountain whites of the South, that mete out a rude and imperfect form of justice to the wrongdoer, without the forms of law. Of course this very soon degenerates into the *vendetti* and the son or grandson, down to the third and fourth generation, must avenge the insult or injury of the past, so that after a while the clan or the family makes it its chief business to rob or exterminate some other family that it believes has wronged it. The word *Mafia* means an organization made up of many small gangs called *Cosche*. The *Cosche* is an artichoke, and any one who has eaten an artichoke knows how closely the succulent leaves hug the center, and require considerable force to pull them away. Thus the members of the *Mafia* hold together as closely as the leaves of an artichoke.

We are assured that the *Mafia* "usually lives by blackmailing on the suavest and most courteous lines, and it only resorts to theft and murder when need requires to terrorize the rare refuser of tribute or to punish treachery in its own ranks." The worst feature of the *Mafia*, like the *Camorra*, is its evil political influence. It is so strong in some places that it is said that no deputy can be elected to parliament unless he promises it protection, and that its patrons in the senate and the popular chamber of the Italian government are the worst foes to the honor and integrity of the country.

But while we remember this, we must also not forget that the American cannot throw many stones at the *Mafia* while he remembers the influence the political thugs of New York and Philadelphia have at times exerted at Albany, Harrisburg, and Washington, and while he remembers the lynchings, and the feuds that have been settled by the shot gun and the pistol in the ruder portions of our own country.

It is reassuring to remember that the average emigrant is not drawn from the *Mafia* or the *Camorra* caste. Very few emigrants, good, bad or indifferent, go from Naples to America, though many sail from Naples, while the *Mafia* of Sicily is made up largely of small landed proprietors and petty tradesmen, a class which stays at home, while the poorer, but more honest, day laborer, who has nothing to gain or lose from the *Mafia*, seeks new homes in another continent.

From Sicily, then, as from the rest of Italy, I believe we have very little to fear from the immigrant. He is, to be sure, poor, ignorant and often bigoted, and extremely narrow in his views, but he is enterprising, vigorous, brawny and teachable, and, if we can but bring the influences of the common school and an enlightened church to bear upon him in his new home, he will not make, by any means, the worst American citizen. Our ingenuity and efforts should not be centered upon plans for keeping him out, but upon plans for making him a worthy citizen, since in most of the Sicilian immigrants there is good American timber in the rough.

CHAPTER XVI

EDUCATION AND RELIGION

In some respects Italy takes front rank in the family of the nations in the matter of education. She has several famous universities, some of which, at least, are still worthy of their ancient repute. She has many good technical schools and art is taught as perhaps in no other land save France. But the weak point in Italian education is the elementary school, the school which more directly affects the people with whom we have to do in this volume. Few emigrants have a university education, and not many have taken a course in science or art, so that except indirectly, in furnishing a sort of national ideal, which undoubtedly to an extent affects the common people, the emigrant is not greatly indebted to the higher schools.

In what we should call the primary and grammar grades, Italy has been in the past woefully deficient, but it is hopeful to know that she recognizes her defects, and is seeking every year to remedy them. Yet it is still true that while money is poured out lavishly for the army and navy, it is doled out to the public schools with a grudging hand.   The education department has been called "the Cinderella of Italian Administration," yet constant progress is being made in primary education.   In the last two decades of the last century the percentage of illiteracy fell from sixty-seven per cent to fifty-six, and if it were not for the handicap of the backward south, especially Calabria and Sicily, the percentage of gain would be much higher, for in the northern and progressive province of Piedmont only twelve or fourteen per cent of the people can neither read nor write, and it is safe to say that every child in the north can receive, and most of them do receive, elementary teaching.

Education, according to the statute books, has been compulsory for more than fifty years, but in many provinces in name only, since neither schools nor teachers enough have been provided to teach all the children even their A, B, C's. The following is a picture drawn by a careful English writer, of the schools of Italy a few years ago:

At least one-fifth of the school buildings are bad,—close, insanitary, over-crowded, frequently unprovided with closets, occasionally placed in stables that have been adapted to the purpose. In whole districts sometimes hardly a school can

boast a building specially constructed for it—
dwelling-houses, suppressed convents, if not
worse, supply the sole accommodation. . . .
Italian schools are liberally staffed as compared
with those of most other countries; but in more
than half the schools a single teacher has to take
three classes, either of boys or girls. In 10,000
schools a master, or more frequently a mistress,
has to teach three classes of both sexes. As a
consequence, the teaching in the great majority of
smaller schools is worse even than that of a bad
village school in England.

The great majority of the teachers are high-
minded men and women, who, poor, over-worked,
ill-treated by the authorities, often barely tol-
erated by their neighbors, make a noble effort to
inform and moralize their truant scholars. But
their capabilities often fall short of their high
purpose, and some have small stuff or training
for their work. . . . If one may judge from the
inspectors' reports, arithmetic (thanks largely, no
doubt, to the use of decimals) is the only subject
taught at all well in the average school. A great
deal of time is necessarily occupied in teaching
good Italian to children, who only speak their
own dialect, and to whom the literary tongue is
almost a foreign language. The quality of the
writing may be judged from the fact that "cal-
ligraphy" is a separate subject only taught in the
upper standards. After the elementary subjects,
and a smattering of natural science taught inci-
dentally with them, the acquirements of the rural

scholar stop short.   In the towns where the upper standards are taught, the pupil learns some
geography and history, and a little elementary
science and geometry.   Drawing is taught by one
teacher in five, but seldom to much purpose.
There are rarely sufficient specimens or apparatus for effective object lessons.   Singing is taught
in many schools, as a rule poorly, but sometimes
well. . . . A certain number of teachers take the
children for excursions, and collect objects for
the school museum.   Gymnastics are an obliga-
tory subject, but they are much neglected, largely
from the want of playgrounds.   The examina-
tions are generally conducted by incompetent local persons, and on no common principle.

I have quoted this extended extract because it
gives a careful, though perhaps not altogether
unprejudiced account of the Italian school, and
because written by authors who have made a long
and careful study of their subject.   If the picture
is dark, it is relieved by the fact that the schools
are on the up grade.   When we remember what
Italy has had to accomplish within the last fifty
years in establishing representative government,
in suppressing brigandage, in establishing and
maintaining and supporting an enormous army
and navy to support her claims as a first class
power, we may well wonder that education has
progressed as it has.

Since the emigrants to America come largely from the south of Italy where the schools are fewest and poorest, only about sixty per cent of them could be admitted under the new law. But this percentage is constantly being increased, and at the present rate it will not be many decades before the Italian emigrant, in the matter of his A, B, C's at least, can take his place beside his Bohemian brother, and his companions in the steerage from the north of Europe.

In the matter of education, the schools of Italy, like our own, are entirely secular in theory. Morals are taught, and morals of a high grade at that, but religious dogma is barred in the schoolhouses, and within school hours. The commissioner of education carefully guards the textbooks from dogmatic bias, though in some of the reading books well selected extracts from the Bible are given, because of their pure literary style and exalted morality. Any one is at liberty to write a textbook and send it to the Board of Education, and, if it passes muster, it is introduced into the schools to a greater or less extent. The higher authorities are evidently awake to the importance of their task, and are doing everything possible, with the means at their disposal, to improve the educational status of the common people.

The religious status of Italy is a difficult subject to treat from an unprejudiced standpoint.
In another book [1] I have paid grateful tribute to
the work of the American missionaries, especially
to the extensive educational and religious propaganda carried on by the Methodist Episcopal
Church of America, and the English Wesleyans
and Baptists.

I have already told briefly the glorious history
of the Waldensian Martyr Church of Italy, the
only indigenous Protestant faith, which is doubtless the hope of the Italy of the future so far as
Protestantism is concerned.

As to the condition of the Catholic Church I
find that opinions differ widely. One man will
tell you that it is decadent to the last degree and
almost moribund; another that since the abolition of the temporal power of the Pope, the
church has gained in enterprise, vigor and spirit-
uality; still another will tell you that Modernism
and the scientific spirit are sapping the power of
the priesthood, while still another will say that
the influence of Modernism has been greatly
checked of late and that it is no longer a serious
menace to the spiritual claims of the Church.

There is no doubt that, with the advent of Pius
X and the present Pope, the Vatican has ap-

1 "The Gospel in Latin Lands."

proached much nearer to the Quirinal. Though
the Pope still keeps up the fiction of being the
"Prisoner of the Vatican," the ecclesiastical authorities practically recognize that Rome is and
will continue to be, the capital of United Italy,
and Catholics are no longer forbidden, as they
once were, to take any part in the politics of the
nation, though Pius X wisely disapproved of the
formation of a Catholic political party.

As to the religious tendencies of the common
people, I find that here, too, opinions differ
greatly.   The extreme Protestant, who, I regret
to say, will tell you that no religion at all, even
infidelity and atheism, are better than the teach-
ings of the Catholic Church, will also tell you that
the Church has lost its hold; that three-fourths
of the people never go to church at all, and that
the few that do go are old women or little children.

I have purposely gone into many Catholic
churches in many parts of Italy for the purpose
of seeing with my own eyes if devotion to the
church is as extinct as we are sometimes told.
I have never been into any Catholic church, large
or small, morning, afternoon or evening, without
seeing some worshippers, apparently earnest and
devout, and during the services the churches are
often crowded, while the proportion of men seems

The Boromean Islands of Lake Stresa

quite as large as in the average Protestant Church. Staunch Protestant as I am, I do not believe that anything is gained by a distortion of facts, or by the unlimited Billingsgate which is sometimes heaped upon the Church of Rome. It is like borrowing the weapons of some of the Romanists themselves, which have proved so ineffectual in their attacks upon Protestantism.

Since the advent of the present century, the Catholic church has gained in Italy, so far as outward prosperity is concerned, for there are hundreds more monks, and some thousands more nuns than at the beginning of the century, and, though many convents and monasteries have been suppressed, their total number has increased by more than eight hundred since the year 1900.

But all these figures, and these conflicting opinions, tell us little of the real spiritual state of the church. It is undoubtedly true that superstition, bigotry and ignorance have flourished in Italy in the past under her ægis. It cannot be denied that she has kept the Bible from the common people and has often encouraged their belief in myths and false miracles. Nevertheless, we may well be grateful for the moral restraints which the Church of Rome throws around its votaries and for the undoubted spiritual life which is nourished in many hearts.

CHAPTER XVII

WILL THEY MAKE GOOD AMERICANS?

The title of this chapter is the most important question which we can ask concerning these new Americans. More important than to know the country from which they come, the history and characteristics of their fatherland, its resources and its needs, is it to know about the people themselves, and whether they have the innate qualities which, under new skies and on a broader field, will develop them into worthy and useful citizens.

What are the characteristics, which, if we could have our wish, we should demand of the immigrant? Are they not these? Industry, thrift, temperance, and the capacity for patriotism. The list of good qualities might doubtless be lengthened, but we think these will embrace the more conspicuous traits which a reasonable man would demand. In good measure I think we shall find that the Italian immigrant fills the bill.

Let my readers consider for a moment what it means to emigrate to a new country, knowing nothing of its language, its customs and its laws. Even an educated traveller, armed with his phrase book and his indispensable Baedeker, does not feel altogether at his ease, when he steps ashore on new soil, and the majority of travellers who can afford it, avail themselves of the kindly offices of Cook or some other tourist agency, or hire a courier to see them safely through.

But consider what it must mean for the uneducated peasant, who perhaps can barely read and write his own language, to face the strange, always busy, and often harsh, officials who meet him at the landing stage. He does not understand their sharp orders. Everything is new and strange and often terrifying to him. He has lived, perhaps, in a little country village, knowing only a score of neighbors, and finds himself, after a dozen days in the steerage, dumped down into the midst of a great city, noisy and bustling, full of perils to his unaccustomed senses, and utterly indifferent to him, a poor, lonesome human unit among millions of his kind, who never give him a thought or a second glance. To face such an experience must require pluck and enterprise, and, as a rule, we shall find only the plucky and the enterprising in the out-going steerage.

On this account, as we have watched the long, interminable line of new Americans. waiting for their medical certificates in the great emigration shed at Naples, or at Genoa, we have seen that they are for the most part young men, strong, vigorous, unintellectual perhaps, but with a certain amount of courage and enterprise showing itself in their faces, enough to lead them to face the perils of the deep, and the greater perils of the new land.

It is true that here and there one might have seen an old father or mother, and not infrequently a whole family, wife and children, brothers and sisters, but the staff and stay of these families, you may be very confident, are not weaklings in will or character, however illiterate and uncultured they may be.

But have they not only the courage to face new conditions, but stamina enough to work out their destiny by plodding, patient toil when they reach America? The passing traveller who sees the *lazzaroni* of Naples, basking in the sun on the cathedral steps, and stretching out impotent hands for alms, with scarcely enough vitality to care whether any one gives them a soldo or not, carries home a false impression of rural Italian character. The immigrants do not come to us from the slums of Naples, or from any other great city. Scarcely one in a hundred of them is city born and bred, and these few are for the most part skilled artisans, stone-cutters, or sculptors, or barbers or waiters, for a waiter who can divine the needs of his guests and supply them promptly and deftly, may be considered not only a skilled artisan, but almost an artist.

Such emigrants are comparatively few and far between. The vast majority come directly from the soil, as I have been assured over and over again by inspectors and commissioners who know them thoroughly. They are the small farmers, very small oftentimes; more likely the day laborers who have not an inch of land that they can call their own. But though they smell of the soil, and sometimes show traces of it, they have the virtues of the soil as well; homely, plodding, patient industry. The steam plough has not yet made its appearance in Italy. The reaper, binder, and thresher with motor attachment have not yet reduced the use of a man's muscles to a minimum, and substituted steam and electricity for "elbow-grease." Whatever else these emigrants have or have not learned, they have learned to work, and as one watches the man with the hoe, or the man with the spade in the fields of Italy, or the man with the pruning hooks in her vineyards, he sees that there are no lazy bones in their bodies, or, if there are, these members receive very little consideration.

M. Bazin, like many other travellers, confirms this view when he writes:

This world of poverty is also a hard-working world. I know of nothing more erroneous than that popular prejudice which represents the Italians as a nation of *lazzaroni,* picturesque in their rags, always basking in the sun, always stretching out a hand for charity when the stranger passes by.

Look at those men digging trenches in the rice fields, or at those preparing the ground for the winter wheat, or at those—and the women, too—who are stringing up along the sides of the farm buildings the russet ears of corn, the sheaves of the *gran turco,* of which *polenta* is made. Are they idle over their work? Is there any air of opera peasants about them? I have been among Italian laborers in the great estates at the foot of the Apennines; I have seen them on the Roman Campagna, and the country around Naples, at Reggio in Calabria. In Sicily the French superintendent of the Duc d'Aumale's vineyards assured me that they were more industrious, that they had more endurance and more patience than any French laborers he had ever known. Others have said to me, speaking of Romagna, that I shall see there "the greatest diggers of the ground" that there are in the world. Everywhere, and at all times, the same testimony comes to me in respect to this strong, unhappy race of men.

But we do not need to go to Italy to mark the industry of the inhabitants. The Italian peasant is the *navvy* of the world. He has ousted the Irishman from his former place as digger and ditcher, or rather the Irish-American has risen in the scale and left his old job to the Italian, which indeed he shares to a greater or less extent with the Hungarians and the Slavs from central Europe. Who would build our embankments, and lay our rails, and dig our tunnels, and scoop out our subways, if Italy did not send us the men to do it? It is hardly too much to say that the industrial development of America would be put back a quarter of a century had Italy not opened her doors to let them out, and had we not opened ours to let them in.

Almost any railway journey in America will show us these sons of sunny Italy, brawny if not big, industriously wielding pick and shovel, crowbar or drill, in order that America may develop her resources and fulfill her destiny.

But thrift usually goes with industry, as it certainly does, as a rule, with the Italian emigrant. How could a man live and support a large family on two hundred dollars a year, if he were not thrifty? The very hardness of his lot, and the difficulty of subsistence, have, perforce, made him economical, and economy and thrift are usually synonymous. The housewife will make a cabbage and a knuckle bone go farther than most native Americans would make a loin of beef and half a dozen expensive vegetables.

A walk through an Italian fish market, or a glance at a bill of fare in a *trattoria,* will convince the spectator of the truth of my contention.

In the fish market one will see not only turbot and sole and all the delicacies of the ocean, but devil fish and squid, cuttle fish and octopus, sharks and porpoises, displayed for sale. Nothing is too coarse or repulsive for the Italian peasant to eat, if it is not absolutely poison. On the bill of fare of the restaurant one will find *Fritto mista* and if he orders it he will be surprised to find that squid and octopus, though tough and leathery, are not such hideous things to eat as they are to look at. He will find, too, that an Italian can cook macaroni and polenta in more ways than the most voluminous cook book will tell you how to serve eggs, which, if counted up, will number, I believe, something like thirty-three, and each way of cooking it seems a little better than the last.

A pleasant picture of a fairly well-to-do Italian peasant is quoted from a source unknown to me in "Italy To-day." It must be remembered that this peasant lives in Piedmont, and that the peasant of the south would hardly boast such a varied and comparatively luxuriant bill of fare.

In the morning he works, except in winter, two or three hours before 7.00, when he has a little breakfast of bread and cheese, with capsicums, celery, or radishes in oil, and three-quarters of a pint of thin wine. Breakfast lasts about half an hour. At 11.00 he has dinner from a great round dish of polenta, yellow as gold and smoking like a volcano, or else a *minestra* of macaroni or rice and vegetables, cooked with lard, except on fast days, when oil takes the place of lard. The men sit in the kitchen round the table, the women serve and eat, the boys squat by the chimney or on the doorstep, eating greedily, porringer on knee. If polenta is the dish, the women prepare a sauce, and what sauce it is! Our peasant women all come from the same school of cookery, and all their sauces are made of oil and garlic and anchovy. Sometimes they eat with the polenta a kind of sheep's cheese, and on fast days salt fish, or rarely eggs. With a glass or two of the usual thin wine, dinner finishes. The peasant rises, wipes his lips with his apron or his hand, and goes contented back to work and to digest the two or three big slices of polenta he has inside him. He is never troubled with indigestion, and barely three hours later he is back again to eat his *merenda* of bread and cheese and salad. The *merenda* lasts, like breakfast, half an hour, and like it, it is taken under the shade of a tree. Finally, at dusk he leaves his work and comes home to find supper ready. If they eat polenta at dinner, they eat *minestra* now, and *vice versa*. After supper they go to bed, except a few naughty men, who sit up to have a pipe.

In the matter of temperance few people surpass the Italian peasant. It is true that he is not often a teetotaler, but the sour wine liberally dosed with water which he uses most sparingly is probably little more intoxicating than a cup of coffee.

Even the light wine which his vineyards produce in such abundance is drunk by the peasants but very sparingly, chiefly, perhaps, because he cannot afford it. The proprietor of a large vineyard on the foothills of Vesuvius assured me that his laborers only drank it on special occasions, perhaps once a week on Sundays, and that then a *mezzo litro,* less than a quart, would suffice for a large family. The Italians will have little difficulty in accommodating themselves to the prohibitory laws which have now so happily been established in America.

I have mentioned the capacity for patriotism as one quality of a desirable citizen, but that the average Italian possesses this quality need not be argued, when we consider the history of mod-

ern Italy which has already been so briefly rehearsed. Men that could rally to the standard
of Garibaldi, that could be so fired with enthusiasm to die for their country, that could endure
privation and hardships untold for a free and
united Italy, will, surely, when they have adopted
the United States for their own, be willing to
live or die for her freedom and unity. However
dull the new immigrant may appear, however
awkward and confused, however little learning of
the schools he may possess, I believe that there
is in him, when awakened, a capacity for genuine
patriotism and true love of country.

CHAPTER XVIII

WHERE THE ITALIAN IMMIGRANT SHOULD SETTLE

The great problem of emigration after all, as has often been remarked, is the problem of distribution. We have not too many foreigners in America, but we have too many in one place. This is particularly true of the Italian immigrant. There are broad fields waiting for him to cultivate; there are prairies that would smile with the harvest, if he should tickle them with the hoe. There are communities that his brawn and energy would arouse from a hopeless stagnation. There are schools that need his children, and he has plenty of children that need the school.

The great question, to which we should address ourselves, is how to bring the man and the work together, nor would this seem to be a hopeless problem, when we have the work needing to be done and the worker waiting to do it. The latest statistics, before the war, of the Commissioner General for Immigration for the United States, tells us that in the fiscal year 1913, something over 274,000 Italians came to our shores, a number far greater than from any other country save Russia, and while the Russians represent many races, Poles, Ruthenians, and Slavs of different tongues, the Italians, both from the north and south, are fairly homogeneous.

But where did this great horde of immigrants find homes? More than 100,000 of them apparently remained in overcrowded New York. Some 24,000 of them settled in Massachusetts, which already has an enormous Italian population, considering her size; 48,000 of them went to Pennsylvania, 12,000 to Connecticut and over 10,000 to Ohio, while over 4000 found their homes in little Rhode Island, which seems already to have as many people to the square mile as is necessary. This accounts for almost three-fourths of all the steerage passengers who left Italy for America in the year 1913, leaving barely one-third for all the other forty-two states, to say nothing of Alaska and the island territories of the Union.

Not one of these states, save Ohio, is preëminently an agricultural region. The Italians have evidently settled down largely in the great centers, like New York, Philadelphia, Boston, Providence, and Cleveland. Yet these immigrants were not city dwellers, for the most part, before they came to America.

Another table of statistics tells us that they were largely farm laborers and servants. They have come from the soil of the old world; they should seek the soil of the new.

It is true that a certain number of them, perhaps tens of thousands in the aggregate, are still needed to build our railway embankments, and to dig our subways and tunnel our mountains, but, for our own welfare and theirs, the same occupations which engaged their energies in their old home should occupy them in the new.

While New York became the home of 100,000 new Italians in 1913, South Dakota, with its limitless untilled prairies, received just thirty-four, while the sister state of North Dakota furnished a home for only thirty-nine.

If it should be claimed that the Dakotas have a climate so much colder than that of Italy that the sons of the sunny south are not attracted there, we can reply that the southern states fared little better as to the number of Italians whom they attracted. Mississippi was the intended residence of only one hundred and twenty-four Italians in 1913; Arkansas became the home of forty-nine, and the imperial state of Georgia of only fifty-two.

We are reminded by every bakers' and butchers' bill that the cost of living has greatly in-

Capri — The Bertha Krupp Road (So-Called)

creased; that while our population is growing by leaps and bounds, the number of our cultivated acres is almost at a standstill; that while there are every year a couple of million more mouths to feed in the United States, there is, proportionally, every year less grain of our own raising to put into them; that the number of cattle upon our prairies has diminished by millions during the last decade, only since the war showing a slight increase, and that the price of steaks and chops is soaring to such a point that the former necessities of the poor are becoming the luxuries of the rich.

And yet all this time there were coming every year to our shores, from this one country alone, approximately a quarter of a million of agriculturalists, who turned from agriculture as soon as they reached our shores, and sought other employments, which are already crowded, and which other people could perform as well as they.

The Italian, who is a country dweller in Italy, becomes a city dweller in America.   A man who never saw a town as big as Oshkosh, or Tombstone, in his own country, finds himself huddled with tens of thousands of other Italians in the "Little Italy" of New York or Boston or Philadelphia, as soon as he reaches America.

I am fully aware that the wide distribution of

the immigrant, to bring the right job to the right man, is by no means an easy task, but it is one to which I believe our government authorities and our philanthropists should address themselves with the utmost diligence. One of our rich men could not do better than to set aside five million dollars, or ten millions if necessary, for a foundation to seek the solution of this tremendous but most important task.

There is another section of our country, besides the Far West and the South, where the industrious Italian might earn a good living and find a comfortable home; I refer to the abandoned farms of our New England and Eastern states. There are tens of thousands of these which the frugal, hard working sons of Italy could make to blossom like the rose. I know of one town in New Hampshire which is almost absolutely deserted. Schools are abandoned, old highways are grown up with trees and bushes, and dilapidated farm houses stare at us pathetically from the empty sockets of their paneless windows, while the barns and outhouses are tumbling into ruins. This town is more or less typical of many others.

Old orchards which for years have been given up to the ravages of the caterpillar, only need pruning knives and the sprayer to induce them to renew their youth.   With a little repair these homes would furnish the Italian immigrant with a far better place of abode than he ever had in his own country.   His children would have plenty of fresh air and sunlight.   In a few years the schoolhouses would again be filled, the playgrounds would ring with merry laughter, and the ancient highways would again be trodden by the foot of man and beast.

But what do we find when we examine the statistics of immigration to these states?   Two hundred and ninety-two Italians, in 1913, out of the 274,000 found their homes in New Hampshire; three hundred and fifty-six went to Vermont, most of them probably to the marble quarries of Rutland, and six hundred and eighteen found their way to Maine, most of these, in all probability, to the cotton mills of Lewiston and Auburn, of Saco and Biddeford.   It is impossible to tell how many of the 100,000 who made New York their home went into the rural districts, and to the abandoned farms of the Empire State, but it is safe to say that it was an entirely negligible quantity.

Moreover, it must be borne in mind that these Italian immigrants are not simply agricultural laborers of the lowest caste.   They may not be able to read or write, but the very exigencies of their life at home have educated them in many practical directions. Most of them can build a stone wall, or shoe a horse, or make a passable broom out of a handful of bushes, or mend a plough or trim a haystack in a really artistic way. At home, most of them have lived far from professional blacksmiths and masons, and even when it comes to cobbling a pair of shoes, or making a pair of trousers, many of them would be quite equal to the emergency, on so many lines has Necessity conducted their practical education at home.

But above all, they know how to dig and delve, and are not afraid of hard work. "Elbow-grease" has been their chief capital in the home-land and they have brought it all with them. Moreover, they are so thrifty and economical for the most part, that they can live in comfort and almost luxury, as we have already said, where a native American would half starve. What he would consider "slops and dog-meat," the thrifty Italian would consider a nourishing soup and a toothsome ragout.

Macaroni, for instance, is one of the cheapest foods in the world, and on this and polenta, which is practically what we know as hasty pudding, the Italian will grow fat and keep happy. In many parts of Italy macaroni has become a synonym for the staff of life, so that the cab driver, or the waiter in the trattoria, will ask the foreigner, not for *Trinkgeld* (drink money) as in Germany, or *Pour boire* (which means the same thing) as in France, but will ask for *macaroni,* by which he means a soldo or two as recompense for his services.

It may be urged that it would be a long step backward if the country settled by the Pilgrim Fathers, or the sturdy English and Scotch, in past centuries, should pass into the hands of the illiterate Italian, but anyone who has journeyed much through the rural districts of New England, or seen the conglomerate settlements of the Far West, will not be much impressed by this argument.   Some of the most degenerate spots in our country, we are told, are found among the remote New England hills.   Here are found people who live without the law and without the Gospel, who are practically heathen in their beliefs and their actions; communities which every now and then startle us by the commission of some unnatural crime, and which are degenerating from year to year.

The infusion of some red Italian blood into these communities would do them no harm, for it must again be remembered that it is not the degenerate Italian who emigrates.   Such an one has neither pluck, enterprise, nor stamina to do so, even if he could pass the immigration officials. However ignorant the emigrant may be, his keenness of intellect is often beyond dispute. Any traveller in Italy will testify to the sharpness of the Italian newsboy or postcard vendor. He can pick out a foreigner in a crowd of ten thousand people; he can differentiate an American from an Englishman, and will be sure to offer the former the Paris *New York Herald,* and the latter the Paris *Daily Mail,* and if any Yankee can get the better of him in a bargain for his pictures or his trinkets he is welcome to do so. The farmer class, too, from whom we draw our immigrants so largely, though not so vivacious are by no means fools.

If it is further objected that an alien religion would thus be introduced into the old communities of the English and Dutch Pilgrim Fathers, it may well be replied that an alien religion is better than none, and according to the reports of our Home Missionary Societies, many of the decadent communities have not only lost the faith of their fathers, but have not substituted for it any faith of their own.

Thus, from every starting point, we come back to the same conclusion. There is plenty of room for every decent, well-intentioned, able-bodied emigrant from the Old World, and we need them as they need us. We have single states into which the whole population of Italy might be poured without overcrowding it; we have new states that need new workers, and old states that need them none the less. The pressing problem is not solved by exclusion, or even limitation, but by wise distribution.

CHAPTER XIX

THE FUTURE OF THE ITALIAN IMMIGRANT

I do not intend to assume the rôle of a prophet in this chapter, but it does not require the vision of a seer to realize that the mighty flood tide that has been pouring into America from Italy every year and which the world-war has only dammed up for a season, will have no inconsiderable effect upon the fortunes of our country. During the first thirteen years of this century more than two millions and a half of Italian immigrants reached our shores—to be exact, 2,532,240. Few states in the Union have a larger population than this. More Italians have come to America during those thirteen years than would people any one of the great states like Iowa, Georgia, Wisconsin, or Tennessee, while the population of New Hampshire, Vermont, North and South Dakota and Oregon all combined, would not equal the number of Italians who, since this century began its course, crossed the Atlantic to find new homes within our hospitable borders.

It is true, as we have seen, that not a few of these immigrants have gone back to their old home, and some of them have doubtless crossed more than once, so that an allowance for certain duplications must be made in these figures. But at the same time it must be remembered that hundreds of thousands of children have been born of these immigrants since they came to America, and that hundreds of thousands more preceded them during the last century.

Thus, from whatever standpoint we look at it, the problem of assimilating these newcomers is a serious one; to some it would seem an appalling problem.

The writers of "Italy To-day" declare that "from a political point of view the immigration into North America is of comparatively little importance. The Italian finds himself face to face with the Anglo-Saxon and the German, and is handicapped in the fierce competition by his poverty and illiteracy. He is despised as a pauper, suspected by the working classes because of his cheap labor, hated by the Irish, who regard him as an enemy of the Pope. And thus he often loses his nationality, and becomes an undistinguished part of the great alien proletariat. Or, if he retains his love of fatherland, his ambition is to save a little money and return; he has done nothing to raise the status of his class in his adopted country."

But these words were written in the last year of the former century and the latest statistics available for these writers were those of 1898 when only 78,000 Italians came to America, though in that year for the first time the Italian immigration was greater than from any other one country. Since then we have already seen how they have swarmed to our shores. The problem has not only become proportionately greater with the greater numbers, but the status of the Italian immigrant has decidedly changed, and, I believe, for the better. It cannot be said any longer that he is "an undistinguished part of the great alien proletariat." These same writers, in speaking of the Italians in South America, write in a more hopeful vein:

While the Italians as a race have no future in North America, a vast breadth of the southern continent promises in a few decades to be a great Italian country. There are already, it is probable, in Brazil and Uruguay and the Argentine about 3,000,000 Italians in a population of some 23,000,000, of whom the great majority speak Portuguese or Spanish. Their numbers swell with an annual immigration of 110,000, nearly as many as that from all other countries combined; and they are more prolific than the stagnant native population. It is not an extravagant estimate that by the middle of the century there will be 15,000,000 of them, and even if they are not a numerical majority, they will, at all events, be the virile and dominant element. In Brazil there are at least 1,900,000 of Italian blood, possibly many more, and some provinces are peopled almost entirely by them. . . . They are asserting themselves rapidly among the inferior races that surround them. The Portuguese have all the pride and idleness of a decaying people; the half-bloods and freed slaves have small wish or power to aspire. And the Italian, unknown here thirty years ago, has brought a patient industry and a commercial enterprise new to the land.

The chief building firm at Rio, the largest flour-mills in the state, belong to Italians; the banks, the hat industry, the textile manufacturers are largely in their hands. This great State, with an area nearly as large as Europe and of boundless fertility, promises under Italian auspices to rise to a prosperity it has never known.

"What is true or likely to be the future of Brazil, is already happening in Argentina," these authors also assert. But why may not the same things come to pass in the United States? The difference between North America and the southern countries of South America is often greatly exaggerated.

My journeys have taken me to almost all parts of South America, and while some of the northern Republics are unspeakably and hopelessly backward in their development, the same cannot be said of Brazil, Argentina, Uruguay and Chile. The people of these countries would compare favorably with those of many sections of North America. There are no more beautiful or progressive cities in the twin Americas, whose Siamese bond of union has been cut by the opening of the Panama Canal, than are Rio Janeiro and Buenos Aires. Indeed, I scarcely know of a city in the world that can surpass Rio Janeiro for beauty or Buenos Aires for enterprise. If, then, the Italians have made themselves factors of such tremendous importance in the countries to the south of the Equator, why may we not expect them to become of great consequence in the conglomerate life of North America?

If it is true, as it undoubtedly is, that "they own nearly half the commercial firms of Buenos Aires, with a capital of $150,000,000, and more than half its workshops," if it is true that "Italian architects and masons have built the greater part of Buenos Aires and La Plata," why may we not expect them to contribute largely to the commercial and industrial prosperity of North America as well?

It is true that competition may be keener in the north, and better educated races may at first stand in their way of immediate advancement, but it is not to be expected that the Italian immigrant, enterprising, bright and thrifty as he is, though at first handicapped by illiteracy, will always be a hewer of wood and drawer of water. What his ultimate place may be among the many, many races that will make the America of the future, I shall not attempt to predict, but I do not believe we shall find him at the foot of the class.

If I do not pose as a prophet, I certainly do not wish to assume in this volume the rôle of a preacher. I desire that the facts and figures which I have attempted to marshal should speak for themselves. The duty of the American to the immigrant has been pointed out with great plainness and eloquence in many a book and sermon. It would seem that he who runs may read. What agencies besides the church, the school and the friendly neighborhood can solve these tremendous problems?

I, myself, can see hope in no other direction, but I believe that these agencies are sufficient for the task. We have raw material of an excellent grade, as I have tried to show, which after the war will again come to our doors in unlimited quantities every year. If it has not been sifted through as many sieves as were our Puritan ancestors, it is not by any means unwinnowed. The perils, the hardships, the uncertainties of a prospective immigrant's life, winnow out, for the most part, the unambitious and the lazy. The Italian inspectors sift still further the applicants in their search for the diseased or the criminal, and the American inspectors on our own shores pass them through a still finer sieve. In 1913, out of 374,000 immigrants they sent back some 3000 as unfitted to become, for one reason or another, American citizens.

In another chapter I have shown something of the reflex influence of America upon Italy. Millions and millions of dollars go back every year to the little hamlets and farmsteads from which the immigrants come. Better than that, sturdy Christian men often return with new and broader and purer ideas bred in them during their sojourn in a land where there is a church without a bishop and a state without a king, and it is not too much to believe that, with these hopeful influences at work in Italy itself, the future immigrant to America will be of a higher grade than his predecessor.

It must never be forgotten that it is the second generation of the immigrant from which America has most to fear. The generation that has shaken off the restraints of the old country, and does not yet understand that the liberty of his new home does not mean license. It is with this second generation that our work in church and school and community has most to do. The children will practically all attend our public schools. Shall they there learn morality, decency, good manners? Some of them we can influence through our Protestant churches and Sunday schools. Many others will find instruction in Catholic institutions. The social settlements will help others. Still more can be done through community kindness and personal interest of neighbors and employers. A pleasant *Buon Giorno!* (Good morning!) will make the newly arrived immigrant's face glow with gratitude, and fill his heart with a ray of sunshine for the rest of the day.

All these things can be done, but it is my profound conviction that unless, directly or indirectly, we can bring to bear upon them the truths of the religion and the ethics which have made our country stable and prosperous, and have enabled us to weather many a threatening storm, we can never fully solve the problem of the incoming millions and this is supremely the duty of the church.

CHAPTER XX

A HALF PENNY IN NAPLES—BARGAINS OF THE STREETS

(The prices and the wages referred to in this chapter prevailed just before the recent war. Both have risen greatly, but the proportion between the two remains practically the same.)

A friend of mine once set out to find out how many things he could buy in the streets of London for a penny. In a few weeks his penny museum was quite full, with articles ranging from a pair of shoestrings to a miniature Bible, and from a jumping-jack to a second-hand copy of Burns.

Any one who should attempt to buy all the pennyworths in Naples would be confronted with a still more bewildering variety. In fact, the monetary unit in Naples is by no means so large as an English penny. An American cent or an English half penny often seems an extravagance there, and the half penny is divided into five centesimi, and with each minutest coin, if one is so disposed, one can buy something.

196

But we will take the soldo (or five centesimi, or one cent, or half penny) for our purchasing unit, since from the Italian slum point we have decided to become somewhat lavish in our expenditures. Let us wander to the neighborhood of the Porta Capuana, where there is a most tempting display offering itself for the coin bearing the image and superscription of *Vittorio Emanuele Re d'Italia.*

A considerable fish market is in this vicinity, and it is surprising how much fish, if one does not insist upon salmon or sole, can be bought for a soldo. You can get a squid at almost any time for the money, and if squid are plentiful, or you drive a sharp bargain, you can often get two. A cuttlefish, too, with his inky bag intact, or a long red tentacle from an octopus, cut in two in the middle, or a tempting slice of devil fish, or a sculpin, can be had for the same price, for all are fish that come to our net to-day, as well as to that of the Italian poor. You can even buy six minnows as long as your little finger, and a quarter as thick, for the same sum.

The fruit market is hard by the fish market, and here is a still more tempting array. Four little oranges as big as the end of your thumb; two half rotten apples, or one comparatively sound one; nine small peppers, two green tomatoes, six dates, seven English walnuts, nine chest-nuts, all for the same useful coin.

I ought to have remarked before we left the fish market, that we could add to our collection for a single soldo four purple sea urchins, with their bristling spines, nearly a dozen snails, and as many as three star fish whose unpleasant rays sprawl in every direction.

Passing on to the vegetable market, a soldo will tempt the vociferous vendor to give up a head of chicory for our salad course, or a small bunch of carrots, or three of the delicious finochi, or fennel bulbs, which only Italians seem to appreciate, and which I often wish I could find in other lands.

However, we may not be gastronomically in-clined, and so we will go to the Porta Nolana, on a Monday or Friday morning, which our faithful guidebook tells us on those occasions "breaks out in a curious and animated rag fair, where all kinds of old clothes change hands." Indeed, on those occasions the Porta Nolana seems like one vast rummage sale, on a scale so enormous as was never imagined in an American charitable bazaar, where the neighbors all rummage their attics for articles they have no further use for, and load up with articles from their neighbors' attics for which they soon find they have equally little use.

But how can I describe such a gigantic rummage sale as this, where a multitude of articles are priced at one soldo, or two at the most? What in the world will that woman do with those two rusty keys which she is buying for five centesimi? Or where will that piece of scrap iron fit in, that another man is exchanging for the counterfeit presentment of his king? And the rags! Did any one ever see such a varied and miscellaneous assortment? They are not fit for the paper mill. The city authorities ought to have made a huge bonfire of them long ago to avoid infection; but here they are, arranged in piles, or fluttering from hooks or dangling over doorways, foul and disreputable to the last degree. They do not tempt any soldi out of our pockets, but somebody must buy them, and the pitiful poverty which their sale implies is a sad commentary on slum life in Naples.

But there are far more pleasing sights than the rag fair of Porta Nolana and where we can exchange our soldi for things more appetizing. For instance, almost directly beneath the window of my hotel, on the curbstone of the Quai Partenope, a sidewalk restaurant is conducted throughout almost every hour in the day.

Here comes in the early morning a vendor of comestibles, his arms festooned with some great rings of coarse bread, which are only less hard than the curbstone on which he deposits them. Frequently he drops them on the sidewalk, which is by no means as immaculate as a Dutch kitchen, but this little accident offends neither him nor his customers, for he picks them up, cuts the rings into four segments, and then deftly opens up each segment, with his carving knife, taking out a piece of the softer interior, which for the moment he lays upon the curbstone before him. Then from a bright copper saucepan which he has also brought with him, and which steams over an iron brazier, giving forth delicious odors to tempt the passersby, he spoons out some little pieces of stewed meat, accompanied by abundant gravy with which he fills the hollow ring of bread. Then, putting in the plug of soft bread which he had taken out, he ladles some more gravy over the top of it and hands it to the eager customer, who munches it with the utmost satisfaction, while the savory sauce drips profusely over the sidewalk as he eats, in spite of his vigorous efforts to suck up as much of it as he can.

Do not suppose, however, that this delicious meal can be bought for a single soldo. The customer must exchange two of these coins of the realm for such a satisfying breakfast as this.

As I am writing this chapter, it happens to be

a stormy day. The waves of the blue Gulf of
Naples are dashing in upon the quay, sullen and
gray. Every now and then the rain drives down
in torrents, but no such little circumstances as
these interfere with our sidewalk restaurant. It
is nearing the noon hour, and it is doing a rushing
business with the cabmen and others, who have
come from far and near to their favorite *trattoria*.

A policeman has kindly given up his little shelter to the lady who is running the restaurant, for
the proprietor, on account of the rain and the
fierce wind, has evidently delegated the task to
his wife for to-day. The policeman's shelter is
not big enough to contain the proprietress and her
big basket of bread, so she stays out in the rain,
that the bread may be kept dry.

Besides her bread, she had to-day three other
viands, the meaty gravy that I have already described, a plate of hot fish, and a lurid compound
in which tomatoes and peppers evidently play a
more important part than the meat and gravy
with which they are mixed. Thus she can supply the wants of different customers, though the
price is the same for each, the broad copper coin
worth a penny.

In other and meaner parts of the city we shall
find at this hour the same trade going on, though

smaller coins exchange hands for the scraps that are sent out into the street from the restaurants, the scraps which the satisfied customer within has left upon his plate.

And what are those fragments a half inch in length, done up in dirty white paper, which a ragged specimen of humanity is offering to sell, a dozen of them for a soldo? We look closer and see that they are cigarette ends, most of which contain but the minutest fraction of tobacco. If this evening we were to take a walk through the streets, we shall see this same man scanning carefully every inch of the sidewalk as he slowly moves along with a lantern in his hand, and every now and then stooping to pick up one of these tempting morsels from the gutter. These night prowlers are *mozzonari,* and they do not despise other treasure trove, besides cigar and cigarette ends, which come in their way.

The goats and the cows will contribute something for our soldo, if we wish a drink of unpasteurized milk, and are not too squeamish about the milkmaid. Often the milkmaid is a man, and, if you wish, he will drive one of his goats up four or five flights of stairs and milk it before your eyes into a bottle with an incredibly small neck, though he seldom seems to lose a drop of the fluid.

Lugano and Mt. S. Salvador

If he is the owner of a cow, he cannot conveniently drive her upstairs, but stands on the sidewalk below, while the customer in the fifth story lets down a basket with a glass or bottle in it, into which the owner of the cow deftly squirts an exact soldo's worth of milk, and, putting it into the basket, it is hauled up by the waiting customer in the fifth story.   But unless she keeps a sharp watch, she is as likely to get adulterated milk as by the system of delivery in other lands, for I have seen one of these cowherds slyly fill the glass half full with water and thus apparently give his customer a very large soldo's worth.

While we are, in imagination, spending our soldo, we see all sorts of trades and family occupations engaging the attention of our friends who dwell in the slums.   Cooking and washing, tinkering and shoemaking, hair cutting and shaving, and the innumerable duties connected with a large family of children, all take place in the open street without a thought or a sign for the blessing of privacy!

But how can any privacy be enjoyed by these people who live in a single room lighted only by a door, as the majority of people in Naples live, who must perform all their household duties and work at their trades in the one room where they must sleep and eat and cook and work, if they do these things under cover? It is easy to see how they are driven to the street or the sidewalk for most of their waking hours.

The sad thing about hunting for a pennyworth in Naples is the terrible poverty which it reveals, for a soldo is as hardly earned as it is hardly spent. Little children must work all day long for four or five soldi. A grown man working twelve hours a day will often make not ten times as much. A woman gets but twelve cents for sewing up the seams of a dozen coarse undershirts, and must furnish the thread herself. A child is paid two centesimi, two-fifths of a cent, for preparing the wicks for a thousand little candles, such as are burned by the million in the churches of Naples. These prices show why a soldo must be stretched to its utmost limits by the poor of Naples, and why the rag fairs and the sidewalk restaurants and the *mozzonari* flourish everywhere in picturesque Naples.

CHAPTER XXI

A TALK WITH DR. GOODHEART, INSPECTOR
OF EMIGRANTS

"America! America! This is the magic word
which attracts hundreds of thousands of immigrants from all parts of the world, to this land
discovered by an Italian—Cristoforo Colombo."
This is the translation of the opening sentence of
the emigrants' *vade mecum,* which is given to
every steerage passenger who will accept it, by
the Waldensian missionaries, as his fellow countrymen are about to embark for the new world.

"*L'America e una terra di lavoro. Il denaro
non si trova sulle stradda.*" (America is a land
of labor. Money is not found in the street.)
This is another illuminating sentence which follows soon after the opening panegyric.

It will not be seriously disputed, perhaps, at
least in the United States, that the encomiums of
this little booklet are deserved, and that America
is the hope of the Italians, but a more serious
question from our own standpoint may be suggested. Are the Italians the hope of America?

Many would answer this with a decided negative, and it must be confessed that the traveler who lands at Naples and drives to his hotel past the unsavory slums that line much of the way will decide that the Italians are the menace and not the hope of America.

However, let us look into the matter a little further, and let me introduce you to my friend, Dr. Buonacorda, inspector of emigrants at the port of Naples, who during the past sixteen years has examined hundreds of thousands of his fellow countrymen, and sent most of them on their way rejoicing, with a clean bill of health. The delightful doctor's name, we might appropriately make over into English, and call him "Dr. Goodheart."

It must also be confessed that he has sent some tens of thousands back to their homes, hopeless and discouraged, because of some disease, usually trachoma, which bars their entrance to the paradise of the new world. But he assured me that of those whom he had passed as worthy of admittance to America, not more than two or three in a thousand had been deported after their arrival at Ellis Island, and these because they had been impersonated by someone else, or for some other fraudulent practice.

When we first see Dr. Goodheart, he is examining the eyes of some four or five hundred would-be American citizens, and with incredible swiftness is lifting up their eyelids, looking for signs of the dread disease and passing them on, most of them happy that the first ordeal is over. He pats the frightened little children on the cheek, and chucks the boys under the chin, and has a pleasant word for the mothers, as the seemingly unending line is marshalled before him.

I must say that I was very happily disappointed in those whom I saw at this fountain-head of the endless stream of emigration from Italy. Three-fifths of them at least, perhaps two-thirds, were young men, strong and sturdy peasants, smelling of the soil, it is true, but totally unlike the scaly ragamuffins of Naples who would make one shudder if he thought they were to be his future fellow citizens.

Occasionally in the long line would come an old man or woman, grizzled and bent, but almost invariably flanked on one side or the other by a stalwart son or daughter, or, perhaps, with good money in their pockets, sent from America by prosperous children, who had assumed the support of the old folks. Not a few young women, too, were there, brides or prospective brides, some of whom showed by their blushes and coy glances that they were "keeping company" with the husky young farmers who preceded them, or followed them in the line.

There was also a goodly sprinkling of children in the throng, rosy-faced boys and girls, for the most part, as dear to their parents as any curled darlings of Fifth Avenue, for the Italians are noted for their gentleness and tenderness to their children.

And here is a little group that has an indefinable air of difference from the others. The mother is a wholesome looking woman of forty years of age, or thereabouts, holding a chubby baby in her arms, and followed by four small boys ranging in age from four to ten. They are somewhat better dressed than the average of their companions, but it is not in their clothes, but a certain bright look of independence and interest in all that is going on around them, that attracts us.

"Where do you come from?" asks Dr. Buonacorda, of the oldest boy, for our benefit. "We are Americans," he proudly answers, and his mother confirms his statement by telling us that all the children were born in America, that they live in Orange, New Jersey (O-rhange, she pronounces it), and that they have just been making a little visit in Italy with the old folks.

The long queue winds on and on, like some

huge boa constrictor that has doubled on itself half a dozen times. But before long Dr. Goodheart interrupts his labors long enough to take me to the office of the chief commissioner of immigration, and, doing most of the talking himself, puts at my service some of the facts with which his sixteen years of inspection have made him familiar.

I wish I could reproduce his emphatic gestures, with which he underscores every sentence, now ticking off each fact on the five fingers of one hand with the five fingers of the other; now shaking his index finger in dangerous proximity to the end of my nose, to emphasize some fact that seems to him of peculiar importance; now shrugging his shoulders until his ears are almost hidden, and throwing out his hands, palms upward, in a deprecatory fashion and shaking them most violently.

Though he does not bear in mind the suggestion in the *vade mecum* before alluded to, "We would recommend to our fellow countrymen when in America not to vociferate or gesticulate when they are talking," yet we would not have his gestures a whit less violent, for they all indicate the utmost kindliness and good nature, and a desire to place at our disposal the largest number of facts which his somewhat limited English vocabulary will permit. Please consider every answer to a question of mine to be punctuated and put in italics or upper case type by his animated countenance, his sparkling eyes and gestures violent enough to be equivalent to a good hour's exercise in a gymnasium.

"Where do these men come from?" I asked.

"All from the country," said he. "None go from Naples or the large cities except the skilled workmen, like barbers, stone cutters, sculptors, and such people. These men are all agricultural laborers. But of course they can do many other things besides dig in the soil. Most of them live far from any large center, and they have to be their own blacksmiths and masons and carpenters and wall builders. What you call 'jack of all trades'? No?"

"But what about their morals," I asked.

"They are most moral," he answered, and, rolling up his eyes toward heaven and lifting his hands skyward, he continued, "Their women are holy in their eyes. A man may bury his knife in his wife's bosom, if he thinks her unfaithful, but it very rarely happens. Divorce is unthinkable. Yes, unthinkable," he repeated, with a violent gesture that swept the very idea out of existence. "When the men go off to America for years, the wife always remains faithful, and then they send

at last for wife and children when they have made
money enough to keep a home."

"Do they often come back to stay?" I asked.

"Not to stay; not to stay," he replied. "They
come back for a little while to visit the old father
or mother, or to look after their little property,
but they usually go back, for the manner of living,
the customs, the wages and everything else in
your great America are so different that they are
never contented to stay here."

Then the good doctor linked the thumb and
first finger of his right hand into the thumb and
first finger of his left, and pulled violently on the
two links, to show how inseparably Italy and
America were bound together by this constant
stream of Italians that are passing back and forth,
back and forth, between the two continents on
every steamer that leaves their shores and ours.

If my readers are interested in statistics, Dr.
Buonacorda could tell them that in 1912-13, the
last full year before the war dried up the stream
of emigration, there were examined by port inspectors 168,189 would-be emigrants, of whom
10,218 were rejected, about 8500 of these being
refused passage on account of trachoma, or suspected trachoma, the other 1500-odd from other
causes.

Naples is one of the three Italian ports from which emigrants are allowed to depart, Genoa and Palermo being the other two.

"What is the average age of the emigrants?" I asked.

"The great majority are from eighteen to thirty years old," replied the doctor, and he did not need to add that these young men were, as a rule, the healthiest and the most enterprising from the district from which they come. Their health is guaranteed by the inspection; their enterprise by the very fact that they were willing to brave the perils of the sea and the uncertainties of life in a new continent, and to turn their backs on their old homes.

Let any one of my readers imagine what it would be for him to tear himself up by the roots and transplant himself to a new hemisphere, where he knew nothing of the language, the customs or the habits of the people, where he must begin life again, and build from the very foundation. Who would not shrink from such an ordeal? Few besides the vigorous and the enterprising would be equal to it.

I will not say that my Dr. Goodheart was not an optimist concerning his countrymen, and that some of his statements were not rose-colored;

but from what I saw and heard that morning in the inspection pen of Naples I concluded that the sons of sunny Italy, if not the chief hope of America, are by no means a serious menace.

CHAPTER XXII

THE WAR AND ITS EFFECT ON ITALY AND ITALIAN IMMIGRATION

One need not be a prophet to foresee some of the inevitable results of the world war upon Italy and the Italians.

A new alignment of the nations has already taken place. Italy has broken forever with her old allies, Germany and Austria. She cast in her lot, on one of the most critical days of history, with the democratic nations to which, in spirit and by her traditions, she has for centuries belonged.

She is one of the most important factors at the peace table of Versailles.

Her boundaries are enlarged by the inclusion of *Italia Irredenta* and she has emerged from the conflict stronger than ever, and with a higher rank among the great nations of the world. It is too soon, as I write, to set down the exact bounds of the Italy of the future, but we can at least say with all confidence that her courage and persistence in snatching victory from defeat, her wise choice of allies in spite of a tremendous and in-

sidious German propaganda, the awakening of
her people through contact with other armies, and
the consciousness of fighting for a just and win-
ning cause, will make her a greater and more
virile nation than she has ever been.

The war, too, has been a great quickener of the
resourcefulness and inventiveness of her people.
In airplane inventiveness, and in some features
of artillery and submarine manufacture, Italy
has been surpassed by none of her allies.

In intrepidity and courage, too, the Italians
have given place to none, as witness the advance
of her armies over the Austrian Alps, coming
almost within sight of Trieste, and the cutting
out and destruction of two great Austrian war
ships within the well-guarded harbor of Pola.

In post-war times, when once more spears are
beaten into plowshares and swords into pruning-
hooks, when the longed-for League of Nations is
consummated, this inventiveness and resourcefulness will be turned into peaceful channels and
other great scientists will arise to rival, and perhaps surpass, the records of those who have already made Italy so renowned.

But will emigration to America from Italy still
continue as in the past?

From all countries in the year ending June 30,
1918, only 110,618 immigrants came to America,

the smallest number, with the exception of one year in the Civil War, since 1844.

In the same year 94,855 aliens returned to their native shores, leaving a net gain for America of only 15,763.

Immigration has practically ceased, but how about the coming days? Doubtless, for a time, the great stream of arrivals from foreign shores will be checked—but only for a time. The return of our own demobilized army may supply the demand for labor for a few years, and Italy and other countries may need all their able-bodied men to build up their own waste places.

A few years, at the most, will be sufficient with this robust race, who have never forgotten God's command to Adam to "be fruitful and multiply and replenish the earth," to restore pre-war conditions.

Though Italy has gained more elbow room she cannot enormously enlarge her contiguous territory. Her relations with her Slavic neighbors, and the more Christian views that will prevail of the rights of small nations, will doubtless prevent her from vastly increasing her boundaries at the expense of her neighbors in Albania and the Adriatic littoral, and the day will soon come when her sturdy sons will again seek the New World which an Italian discovered.

They will be welcomed, I believe, more cordially than ever before, for the common fortunes of war, and the consciousness that Americans and Italians have fought side by side for the same great cause of human liberty, will open our hearts to them and theirs to us as they have never been opened in the past. No longer shall any but the meanest among us think of them as "Dagoes," and desire only their sturdy muscle in building the new America.

More than ever in the past they who have been our brothers in arms will be our brothers in peaceful service, companions in a new democracy that has been made safe for the world because founded on principles of righteousness and justice and fair dealing, individually, commercially and industrially between man and man.

THE END

The Italian American Experience

An Arno Press Collection

Angelo, Valenti. **Golden Gate.** 1939

Assimilation of the Italian Immigrant. 1975

Bohme, Frederick G. **A History of the Italians in New Mexico.** (Doctoral Dissertation, The University of New Mexico, 1958). 1975

Boissevain, Jeremy. **The Italians of Montreal:** Social Adjustment in a Plural Society. 1971

Churchill, Charles W. **The Italians of Newark:** A Community Study. (Doctoral Thesis, New York University, 1942). 1975

Clark, Francis E. **Our Italian Fellow Citizens in Their Old Homes and Their New.** 1919

D'Agostino, Guido. **Olives on the Apple Tree.** 1940

D'Angelo, Pascal. **Son of Italy.** 1924

Fenton, Edwin. **Immigrants and Unions, A** Case Study: Italians and American Labor, 1870-1920. (Doctoral Thesis, Harvard University, 1957). 1975

Forgione, Louis. **The River Between.** 1928

Fucilla, Joseph G. **The Teaching of Italian in the United States:** A Documentary History. 1967

Garlick, Richard C., Jr. et al. **Italy and Italians in Washington's Time.** 1933

Giovannitti, Arturo. **The Collected Poems of Arturo Giovannitti.** 1962

Istituto di Studi Americani, Università degli Studi di Firenze (Institute of American Studies, University of Florence). **Gli Italiani negli Stati Uniti** (Italians in the United States). 1972

Italians in the City: Health and Related Social Needs. 1975

Italians in the United States: A Repository of Rare Tracts and Miscellanea. 1975

Lapolla, Garibaldi M. **The Fire in the Flesh.** 1931

Lapolla, Garibaldi M. **The Grand Gennaro.** 1935

Mariano, John Horace. **The Italian Contribution to American Democracy.** 1922

Mariano, John H[orace]. **The Italian Immigrant and Our Courts.** 1925

Pagano, Jo. **Golden Wedding.** 1943

Parenti, Michael John. **Ethnic and Political Attitudes:** A Depth Study of Italian Americans. (Doctoral Dissertation, Yale University, 1962). 1975

Protestant Evangelism Among Italians in America. 1975

Radin, Paul. **The Italians of San Francisco:** Their Adjustment and Acculturation. Parts I and II. 1935

Rose, Philip M. **The Italians in America.** 1922

Ruddy, Anna C. (Christian McLeod, pseud.). **The Heart .of the Stranger:** A Story of Little Italy. 1908

Schiavo, Giovanni Ermenegildo. **Italian-American History:** Volume I. 1947

Schiavo, Giovanni [Ermenegildo]. **Italian-American History:** The Italian Contribution to the Catholic Church in America. Volume II. 1949

Schiavo, Giovanni [Ermenegildo]. **The Italians in America Before the Civil War.** 1934

Schiavo, Giovanni E[rmenegildo]. **The Italians in Chicago:** A Study in Americanization. 1928

Schiavo, Giovanni [Ermenegildo]. **The Italians in Missouri.** 1929

Schiro, George. **Americans by Choice:** History of the Italians in Utica. 1940

La Società Italiana di Fronte Alle Prime Migrazioni di Massa. (Italian Society at the Beginnings of the Mass Migrations). New Foreword (in English) by Francesco Cordasco. 1968

Speranza, Gino. **Race or Nation:** A Conflict of Divided Loyalties. 1925

Stella, Antonio. **Some Aspects of Italian Immigration to the United States:** Statistical Data and General Considerations Based Chiefly Upon the United States Censuses and Other Official Publications. 1924

Ulin, Richard Otis. **The Italo-American Student in the American Public School:** A Description and Analysis of Differential Behavior. (Doctoral Thesis, Harvard University, 1958). 1975

Valletta, Clement Lawrence. **A Study of Americanization in Carneta:** Italian-American Identity Through Three Generations. (Doctoral Dissertation, University of Pennsylvania, 1968). 1975

Villari, Luigi. **Gli Stati Uniti d'America e l'Emigrazione Italiana.** (The United States and Italian Immigration). 1912

Workers of the Writers' Program. Work Projects Administration in the State of Nebraska. **The Italians of Omaha.** 1941